THE CHRISTIAN RESPONSE TO HOMOSEXUAL "MARRIAGE"

THE CHRISTIAN RESPONSE TO HOMOSEXUAL "MARRIAGE"

How Progressives are Ending America

by

TERRY A. LARSON

THE CHRISTIAN RESPONSE TO HOMOSEXUAL "MARRIAGE"

World Ahead Press is a division of WND Books. The views and opinions expressed in this book are those of the author and do not necessarily reflect the official policy or position of WND Books.

Scripture taken from the HOLY BIBLE, NEW INTERNATIONAL VERSION® NIV®. Copyright © 1973, 1978, 1984 by Biblica, Inc.™. Used by permission of Biblica, Inc.™. All rights reserved worldwide.

Paperback ISBN: 978-1-944212-94-0
eBook ISBN: 978-1-944212-95-7

Printed in the United States of America
16 17 18 19 20 21 LSI 9 8 7 6 5 4 3 2 1

DEDICATION

This is a record, my attempt to explain what happened; so I write this for my children. They have been the wellspring of joy in my life; and I will continue to thank Him for Lily, Connor, Sean, Aidan, and Lydia every remaining day that I have.

CONTENTS

PREFACE

This book was originally titled *The Christian Response to Obergefell v. Hodges*. But a good friend suggested I change the title, since most people who saw that book on a shelf might pass it by because they don't know what *Obergefell v. Hodges* is.

Obergefell v. Hodges is the opinion of the Supreme Court of the United States delivered on June 26, 2015, which is said to have made homosexual marriage legal in all states.

Conflict between Christians and homosexual marriage advocates began several years before *Obergefell*, and afterward it was expected the conflict would grow.

The Supreme Court pulled the same stunt with *Obergefell v. Hodges* that it had with *Roe v. Wade*, declaring state laws were unconstitutional, and making abortion and now homosexual marriage legal in all states. The Court told us what the law is regarding abortion and marriage; the Court gave us the law.

Americans have responded to *Roe v. Wade* since 1973. Most Americans chose to forget about *Obergefell v. Hodges* by the weekend after the opinion was announced.

As I will explain, if Christians—if all Americans who still have any regard for our Constitution—do not yet respond to *Obergefell,* then we are done with our Constitution and we are done with this constitutional republic.

We must not allow this Supreme Court opinion to be enforced as law in those states which only recognize heterosexual marriage under state law.

INTRODUCTION

Early in the last week of September 2016, I took down my SCOTUSProject™ website. I was thoroughly frustrated, sickened, and angry. By the end of the week I had watched a recorded event which only made matters worse.

In his *Socrates in the City* series, Eric Metaxas interviewed the British journalist Peter Hitchens about Hitchens' book, *The Rage Against God*.[1] Both are educated, professing Christian men. I was struck by how widely both missed the mark in their considerations of homosexual marriage.

Hitchens described the destruction of marriage by the divorce laws of the 1960's. He referred to the Christian fight against same-sex marriage as a "futile Stalingrad," because Christians should have defended marriage long before same-sex marriage (the term he uses).

"Who cares?" he asked, if homosexuals marry; when you consider how so many heterosexual marriages have ended in divorce, and many of us no longer marry at all.

Metaxas suggested the impact on the religious liberties of those opposed to homosexual marriage may also be more important than marriage between homosexuals.

I agree with both that marriage between homosexuals, in and of itself, is not the greatest harm or the most important issue we face here. Homosexuals will continue to engage in homosexual behavior, having what they describe as sex with each other, whether they are encouraged to do so through marriage or not. They will live out their lives, refusing to consider that their behavior is sinful according to the Bible and to repent and turn away from it, and spend eternity in hell. They are free to live as they choose. But homosexual marriage normalizes homosexual behavior, and there are more people who will be encouraged to engage in homosexual behavior as a result of sanctioning those "marriages" than people who will be happily married as a result.

Worse, gender nonconformity is being normalized with astonishing speed; and could not have been, if we had not finally and fully normalized homosexual behavior by sanctioning it through marriage. The advocates for gender nonconformity follow the trail blazed by progressives and their homosexual activist tools. The same people who lied and deceived for decades to compel Americans to accept homosexual behavior are on a blitzkrieg to normalize gender nonconformity; with a simultaneous idiotic civil rights movement and demands that girls share bathrooms, locker rooms, and showers with boys in government schools.

I have heard, too often, Christians begin discussions of homosexuality and homosexual marriage with a recognition of the failure of Christians or the church to support and defend marriage. Professing Christians have sex outside of marriage, or end their marriages in divorce, so we should apologize for that before we say anything about homosexuality.

For decades, people with contempt for marriage, only because it is a traditional, largely Christian institution in America; have declared that more than half of all marriages end in divorce only to encourage those who are considering divorce to go through with it. Everyone else does, so you may as well too.

In the churches I have attended since becoming a Christian in 1995, I would guess that ninety percent of the people in the pews are married or will be. Very few people sit alone as a result of a divorce. While too many in the church have divorced, the people in the pews in this country are the only ones who continue to take marriage seriously and to recognize its vital importance for our society.

Homosexual marriage should have been a Stalingrad battle for Christians in America. It should have been the turning point in the American culture war, as Stalingrad was for the Russians in World War II. But Christians in America couldn't be bothered to show up for the fight. So progressives in America met with little or no resistance, unlike the Germans who inevitably lost the war after they lost Stalingrad.

While Hitchens describes the harm done as a result of the failure of Christians to adequately defend marriage for decades before *Obergefell v. Hodges*, it is worse than that. Those Christians continued in their ignorance, indifference, and apathy until they just couldn't be bothered at all to do or say anything about homosexual marriage when that came along.

The consequences of homosexual marriage will be worse than the consequences of heterosexual divorce. So when Metaxas considers the impact of homosexual marriage on religious liberty, on Americans' First Amendment right to our freedoms of religion and of speech, he is a little short of the mark in my opinion. As it is being applied and enforced, homosexual marriage is a deathblow to our Constitution and our republic. It is the second of three deathblows I describe in chapter ten.

In *If You Can Keep It: The Forgotten Promise of American Liberty*, Metaxas warns we are in danger of losing our republic. He describes Os Guiness's "Golden Triangle of Freedom" by which we understand the necessary relationships between faith, virtue, and freedom. There is no freedom without faith and virtue because these are what enable us to be self-governing.[2]

Metaxas does not recognize the republic is already lost. Americans are done with faith, done with virtue, and consequently done with freedom. If Americans were to do anything to attempt to keep our republic, if there was to be some effort to hold a constitutional line, it had to finally begin as a response to *Obergefell*. But Christians across America disregarded and dismissed *Obergefell*, and we will all find ourselves subject to dreadful consequences as a result.

Terms in this Book

I refer to the Supreme Court of the United States as SCOTUS or the Court; and the *Obergefell v. Hodges* opinion delivered on June 26, 2015, as *Obergefell.*

I use the terms *pastor* or *people in the pulpit* in these pages to include Christian church leaders or clergy whose titles might otherwise be Reverend or Father, since most I have interacted with are titled Pastor. I refer to *laypeople* or *people in the pews* for those of us they are responsible to lead.

CHAPTER 1

THE PETITION

The Wisconsin petition is in the Appendix at the back of this book.

For over a year, beginning in August 2015, I discussed the petition with church leaders and laypeople in Wisconsin. This included five state leaders of different Protestant denominations I am familiar with.

I was told what I was doing was political; and a pastor's job is to preach the gospel, not to get involved in issues like this. The petition would have simply enabled Christians who don't want to be involved in homosexual marriages to defend themselves; to reply that state law does not require them to be involved in a homosexual marriage, no matter the opinions of some of the members of the Supreme Court. But the leaders I shared it with didn't see it that way. The petition was going nowhere so I put it aside, and watched as there was no effective response to *Obergefell.*

I am aware of only two pastors who made the petition available for the members of their church to consider. As I recall, I didn't even ask one of them—he just indicated immediately after reading the petition that he would offer it to members the following Sunday. I was blessed with, and encouraged by, his guidance and assistance through the following year.

None of the state leaders would forward the petition to pastors to consider making it available for church members. I didn't want anyone to press anyone else to use the petition, only to make it available for other Christians to consider. Some of the pastors I approached immediately declined; most had to be asked repeatedly and had to discuss it with other pastors or elders before they would do anything with it.

There was nothing wrong with that, of course—a pastor should discuss something like this before involving church members. But I was never contacted again by any of them. I don't recall talking with any laypeople who didn't find the petition agreeable. But leadership, at all levels, would have little to do with it. In the end I found five pastors who signed the petition as a group, and it was printed in a local newspaper.

I wanted the petition read by every Christian in Wisconsin, whether or not they used it by signing and mailing copies to the state's Governor and Attorney General. I wanted every Christian to read and consider it. I wanted every Christian to decide and declare before God, and Man if they used the petition, whether they would go along with this homosexual marriage rot or not.

My task was to get my brothers and sisters in Christ to consider the petition. So I have nothing to say about a decision by a sibling to sign or not sign the petition, or the reasons they had for doing so. But I do have a few things to say about the responses of Christian "leaders."

(1.1) PULPIT MICE

I confess I was disappointed. I met most of these people for the first time when discussing the petition with them, so had no basis for expecting anything. But they were in leadership positions (denominational; as pastors, elders or other leaders) so I expected a bit of leadership attitude or behavior nonetheless.

Most of these people are paid to lead, that is to do or to say something. They are respected because they hold leadership positions. Their function is to respond to something like a SCOTUS opinion requiring Christians across America to be involved in homosexual marriage. They don't have to respond with a petition; but they should do or say something. They are not in leadership positions to follow others; if they are followers they shouldn't be in leadership positions.

I confess I was angered. The widespread cowardice I met with still makes me angry. If some of these leaders had said, "I don't think I like you or the way you look, Mr. Larson," I could have accepted that. But I could smell the fear on some of these people.

I don't handle embarrassment well, and some of the responses were so embarrassing I still feel a little sick to my stomach thinking about them. Some of those leaders, and readers at this point, would accuse me of judging others. So be it. I'm prepared to answer to Him for it some day.

Some of those leaders would be offended, indignant, and defensive; wanting to take me to task after reading these pages. I can accept that. I expect most will not be angry—I believe all are better Christians than I am, clearly intent on determining and doing what they believe is God's will in their leadership positions.

But they should have been a little more offended, indignant, and defensive; they should have done or said something when confronted with *Obergefell.* They should have responded to that more effectively than they did, if they did respond at all.

I should not have come along to write these pages.

Most would not forward the petition to laypeople because they were afraid of something. Some of the people in their pews might endorse homosexual marriage. Some would accuse a pastor of getting involved, or trying to influence others' decisions, in "political matters."

But these people nearly always accuse a pastor only when espousing views they disagree with. They are not sincere or credible enough to accuse a pastor of wrongdoing when they agree with the pastor's viewpoint on "political matters." These people should be disregarded or shown the way out of the church to ply their accusations elsewhere, after any who endorse homosexual marriage.

We would not be in the mess we are in if there were not so many mice in the pulpits in America. The mice I encountered had their reasons for offering little response, or no response at all, to *Obergefell*. I accepted there are things a mouse will do, or will not do, simply because it is in his nature. So when a mouse explained why he couldn't be involved with the petition, I usually moved on to see who was behind the next pulpit.

But there were two responses I could not accept.

(1.2) "IT'S POLITICAL" RESPONSE

Things are described as political by people who "don't want to get involved in politics." Some professing Christians throw the term about, claiming we are not to be involved in politics; then seek to justify their laziness, indifference, or apathy by classifying things as political.

Something which is political can be understood to involve government and its institutions. Some describe government as secular to suggest Christians shouldn't be involved in politics by default, but that doesn't follow. Playing baseball or driving a taxi for a living are secular activities, but no one is reasonably going to argue that Christians should not play ball or earn a living because these are secular activities. Not unless they are living in a monastery.

Government is ordained by God: "Every one must submit himself to the governing authorities, for there is no authority except that which God has established" (Romans 13:1).

We could not live together without some government. Our government was created and established by deists and Christians who believed the moral teachings of the Bible. These moral teachings were put into effect for centuries in law in England before they were applied here. We referenced a *Creator* in our Declaration of Independence, which was followed by our Constitution and our government.

For centuries we understood right and wrong behavior through the moral teachings of the Bible. We established social norms for behavior, unwritten rules which enabled us to live better lives. Through government we enacted laws affirming right and wrong behaviors, including penalties for engaging in those wrong behaviors which had the most serious effects or consequences. Without the Bible we would not have this Constitution and government under which our nation flourished.

Progressives, described in more detail in chapter two, have decided they are to determine what is right and wrong behavior; and they are to run the state (the government), enacting laws to affirm these behaviors. Christians are to have no influence upon the state; not because allowing them some influence is violating a separation principle, but because they may not share progressive values.

Christians declare we are not to be involved in politics, in government; we should give it up for progressives to direct. Christians should not influence government, decisions about what is right and wrong behavior, and the laws which follow. How we live our lives should be determined by progressives, not the outmoded moral teachings of the Bible.

For over a decade, pollsters have declared many Americans believe our country has gone and is going in the wrong direction somehow. Americans are worried about something, but the misdirection is never clearly defined. The wrong direction is the result of progressive control over the direction of the country. Christians and other grown-ups stopped trying to influence, particularly to limit the size of government; and progressives have taken control of that government as they have the educational system, and news and entertainment media. The direction these people have taken the nation has been entirely downward.

Of Course it's Political

I did not understand what feminists meant when I first heard them declaring sex was political in the mid-1980s. What does sex have to do with politics or government?

As progressives worked to tear down the church and any institutions and build up the state to control and direct everything in our lives, all things became political. By the 1980s we had the two political parties engaged in a culture war over social issues. In 2008, we elected a community organizer as president, and students in government schools have joined various progressive political and social movements since then where they act up, act out, and behave like Nazi Brownshirts, as I will describe later.

The politicization of sex led to decades of fighting and legislation on abortion, divorce, homosexuality, marriage, family, and now gender identity. The grown-ups withdrew and let the agitators and juvenile delinquents run the show after the 1960s. Everything was made political and taken up by government to discourage Christians and other grown-ups from resisting the transformation of American culture.

Progressives Take Over

Those who want to end our Constitution and this republic have labored for decades to get God, the Bible, and Christians out of government.

They declared there was no God. They lied about the separation of church and state.[1] They replaced the moral teachings of the Bible with their morality and moral views. They replaced the church with the state. They replaced biblical correctness with political correctness. We "evolved" from holding biblical values to holding progressive values.

Before, we flourished and lived better lives, and people came to understand the value of social norms for behavior, and chose to conform to them without laws or the use of force. Each generation passed these norms and values on to the next. Progressives upended established social norms. They didn't seek to replace them with something better, but to destroy them. All new social norms had to be antithetical to the moral teachings of the Bible—it didn't matter whether they enabled us to live better lives.

Progressives erased all existing norms and standards for sexual behavior. The new norm is no norms, standards or limits. The purveyors of the new social norms have been all about law and force. Too many grown-ups understood these behaviors were wrong to establish them as social norms; thus, behaviors previously discouraged, behaviors not encouraged as social norms, had to be sanctioned by law.

So we had laws to "normalize" aborting babies and homosexual behavior (it was suggested we had laws, but these were merely SCOTUS opinions). Gender disorder or gender nonconformity could not be normalized without law and force, so girls are to be forced to share bathrooms, locker rooms, and showers with boys in government schools.

Progressive hypocrites shrieked for decades about Christian fundamentalists imposing their morality upon others, trying to establish a theocracy. Any efforts to do that pale by comparison to the enforcement of progressive political correctness and the new social norms. These hypocrites confronted well-established laws and social norms based on the moral teachings of the Bible, declared you cannot legislate morality, then set about to legislate everything according to *their* morality.

The further we move away from biblical morality, the more difficult it becomes for us to live together. So the country is split between Christians and others who desire to be left alone to live their lives according to at least some of the moral teachings of the Bible, and those enlightened others who will not leave them be.

(1.3) "PREACHING THE GOSPEL" RESPONSE

When I was a lad, pastors were described as shepherds of flocks. The church members were the flock, and the pastor was the shepherd. It was his function to guide and protect the flock.

I can't find anything in the Bible to indicate preaching the gospel is a pastor's job. They are to preach the Word, by which is meant the Bible in its entirety, but I can't seem to find anything about pastors preaching the gospel. Of course preaching the Bible should include what the Bible says about sexual behavior, homosexuality, and marriage as well as the gospel. There are plenty of directives to proclaim the gospel in the Bible, none of which are limited to pastors. Most directives include a "going out" into the world to spread the gospel. A pastor won't be tending to his flock when he's out in the world proclaiming the gospel. Most pastors have many tasks to perform which don't leave time for work outside their church.

It is the function of the people in the pews to proclaim the gospel. Unfortunately, in America many Christians are afraid to do that, and the most they will do is invite someone to their church where they might hear the pastor preach the gospel.

While some pastors and other church leaders did respond to *Obergefell*, their responses were limited to within their church walls or within the confines of their little group or denomination. Pastors mumbled something in the monthly letters to church members; other leaders shared their thoughts in newsletters or magazines distributed to members of their little cliques.

Every newspaper in the country should have printed a column or a letter to the editor about *Obergefell* from a leader in a local church within a week of the opinion. Every newspaper, so it was understood not everyone was going along with this homosexual marriage rot.

It would have done no harm to at least remind the rest of the country that we are still here, cloistered away in our churches. It would have done no harm to remind the rest of the country that the state is not the only institution in this country with something to say about what is right and wrong.

But hardly anyone could be bothered at the time to do this.

The public didn't hear anyone say "No!" to homosexual marriage in any meaningful way. In the end, everyone went along with it. So the same people who advocated for homosexual marriage understood there would be no opposition, and lunged forward with their next civil rights movement for gender identity.

After *Obergefell* was announced, nearly nobody said "No!" to homosexual marriage. The only mention I noticed was a petition run in a small newspaper by an apparently hateful, right-wing, homophobic and therefore likely Islamophobic individual, signed by several apparently fundamentalist pastors.

Around the same time, in another small Wisconsin town, local parents turned out to say "No!" after leadership in another school district decided that boys who think they are girls must be allowed to use the girls' bathrooms. The district was going along with the Obama administration's suggestion they recognize a right for transgender students to use the bathroom and locker room of choice, or risk the loss of federal funding for local schools.

(1.4) WHAT DOES THE BIBLE SAY?

There are enough Bible verses directing us to be "involved in politics" or government.

We are to submit to "the governing authorities" (Romans 13:1–7). We are reminded of this again in 1 Peter 2:13–17.

We are to make "requests, prayers, intercession and thanksgiving" for those in authority (1 Timothy 2:1–2).

We are to submit to those in authority in government and pray for them.

"Remove the wicked from the king's presence, and his throne will be established through righteousness" (Proverbs 25:5). "When a country is rebellious, it has many rulers, but a man of understanding and knowledge maintains order" (Proverbs 28:2).

When Christians in America have been handed constitutional rights to be "involved in politics" and to influence our government in such a way that those in authority might have people around them who are not "wicked," or in such a way that those in authority do not drive the people toward rebellion against government or God, how can we choose not to do so?

Luke 20:20–26 is often cited to explain why we pay taxes, "giving to Caesar what is Caesar's." We are required to pay taxes if the government requires we do so; government cannot exist without some taxation. Our government is a constitutional republic. We are required to elect people to represent us in the legislative branch of our government. Those who insist Christians should not be "involved in politics" to the point they will not even vote, are undermining our representative form of government, are not doing what is required to maintain and continue it. Being "involved in politics" by voting is no less important than paying taxes. Those people you are able to elect to represent you, are representing you. When they enact unjust or wicked laws, they are doing so on your behalf. You are enacting those laws if you have not at least told your representatives you disagree with them.

While I can point to several verses to indicate Christians are to be "involved in politics" or government,

I cannot find any which prohibit it. For myself, I simply understand "getting involved in politics," and influencing the laws other Americans and their children have to live their lives under, as an act of mercy or pity. I have the ability as a Christian to judge whether laws are unjust, are for good or for evil because of the consequences of those laws, the fruit they produce.

We have no shortage of wicked laws enacted by wicked men, which influence how people live out their lives in this country, including a "law" which encourages people to engage in homosexual behavior, and a "law" which enables a woman to end the life of her baby minutes before it might be born because she must be allowed a choice to do so. Her right to choose is more important than the life of the baby.

When Christians can influence the laws which all citizens must live under, which determine how all citizens will live our lives, how can we choose not to do so?

Finally, consider what has happened because so many chose not to influence government, as progressives demanded. What is the fruit of this?

Our government has been changed from a constitutional republic into a totalitarian state. As I explain later in these pages, the executive branch now makes, applies, and enforces the law. We may as well be living under a monarchy again.

Read 1 Samuel 8, and consider how much we are like the people of Israel.

They followed God and governed themselves. Things went well when they followed God, poorly when they didn't. They had no king. Samuel and those before him had "walked in the ways" of those who came before them. His sons did not follow in Samuel's ways and became corrupt.

Things went poorly for Israel. But rather than returning to walk in the "old ways," to govern themselves by following God, some of the dimwits decided they needed a king to rule over them. God did not want this for the people of Israel. He warned them what would happen under the rule of a king, even that eventually "you yourselves will become his slaves" (v.17). But they would not learn; they refused to listen.

Americans followed God and governed themselves after throwing off the rule of a king and creating this constitutional republic. Things went well; we became an economic and military superpower, the example of liberty and freedom for the world. Then a younger generation decided we would no longer follow God. Rather than walking in the ways of our elders, learning from them and from history, we would do everything differently. Rather than walk in their ways, we would always take the path in the opposite direction, and choose the other fork in the road.

Things went poorly for America as some of the modern-day dimwits decided we needed to be ruled by the state. God did not want this for the people of America or the other free people of the world. We have seen the worst kind of rule by the state with dictators who wanted to rule the world. But we would not learn; we refused to listen.

Samuel warns the people of Israel what will happen to them when they come under rule. Their sons will be taken by the king for war. The king will take from the people a part of the crops they grow; and some of the servants and livestock for himself and his attendants. Finally, "you yourselves will become his slaves." As Americans have come under the rule of the state, we have given up our sons and even daughters for war. The state takes more and more from the people—it is all about taxing and spending. Our children and grandchildren are now indentured servants for life, slaves to our nation's debt.

Choosing to be ruled, when they did not have to be, was unwise for the people of Israel.

Americans have chosen to be ruled as well. We did not have to be. We chose to be ruled when we allowed the federal government to take all powers reserved to the states by the Constitution for itself. We chose to be ruled when we allowed the executive branch to set about making, applying, and enforcing the law. We chose to be ruled when we allowed without question the enforcement of SCOTUS opinions as law.

CHAPTER 2

WHY MUST CHRISTIANS RESPOND TO HOMOSEXUAL "MARRIAGE"?

E veryone who received a passing grade in "Christianity 101" knows there is a God who created us male and female, two to be joined together as one in marriage to be fruitful and multiply. Everyone also knows those things which are done contrary to God's order and plan for His creation are sins. Everyone who passed the class knows we are to avoid sin, and when we do not, repent and seek forgiveness for sin.

So when the Supreme Court of the United States redefines and sanctions marriage as a joining together of two males or two females, encouraging behavior described as an abomination in the Bible, Christians are not to go along with this. Christians are the only people in this country with an obligation to oppose this. If we do not, there is no one else who will.

Most of us took little time to consider the consequences of the *Obergefell* opinion beyond its potential impact on our church. Because we haven't seen the bigger picture, we have not responded rightly. When we see the bigger picture, it becomes clear that every Christian in America must respond to this Court opinion.

Obergefell is about more than homosexuals and marriage and Christians. *Obergefell* is a critical, pivotal victory for progressives in their larger-scale war against the church and against America. I'm including under the progressive umbrella the Marxists, socialists, communists, collectivists, and statists as they are otherwise defined; whose meaning in life comes from tearing down Christianity; and our Constitution, country, and culture.

Progressives were influencing the culture and public policy by the time I was born in the mid-1960s. They were referred to as liberals or the left then. These are the people who championed sex, drugs, and rock and roll. Their fruit was my generation's AIDS, crack babies with mothers addicted to cocaine, and rap, or more aptly described rape music, by the mid-1980s.

By then, *liberal* had become a dirty word; so these people rebranded themselves as progressives, so they could imply their ideology is moving the culture and the nation forward. These people are fluent in Deceit, using word choice to manipulate. People aren't homosexual they are gay; she's not a baby she's a fetus; he's not an illegal alien he's an undocumented worker. In the political arena, things are bipartisan only when they go the way progressives want, otherwise they are divisive.

These people set out to tear down "the establishment" as they called it. They hated their parents' traditional values. They hated Christianity particularly because of its sexual mores, and they declared there was no God. Their fruit includes a massive, controlling government establishment beyond anything our nation's founders could have imagined, with agencies enacting countless rules and regulations. Government is god for these people.

These people have always considered themselves smarter than everyone else. They didn't want to spend their lives in traditional pursuits like working and raising families, so they became civil rights and social activists. The fruits of their labors include a gutter class of rights granted by government to illegal aliens who are not citizens, to criminals in this country and terrorists from other countries, to people who engage in perverse and abnormal sexual behavior, to people who don't know what sex or gender they are, on and on it goes.

I could detail more of the rotten fruit these people have produced, but I expect you know who I am talking about. So let's return to the topic of marriage. Marriage is fundamental to Christianity. Marriage is a foundational, traditional institution in America. Marriage is everything many of these people hate. Progressives encouraged sex outside of marriage, and abortion for the consequences. They advocated for no-fault divorce making it easier to end marriages. In progressive schools of thought it's better to live with someone and have sex before marriage, and having children should be delayed until after career development, both making people less likely to marry.

Whether or not progressives intended to destroy the institution of marriage does not matter; that has been the effect of their influence and their stupid ideas on public policy.

There are plenty of homosexuals who have no interest in homosexual marriage. Homosexuals gain less than progressives through the recognition of homosexual marriage in America. Homosexual activists have been tools for progressives who have been tools for the devil with regard to marriage.

Progressives dominate the entertainment and news media and academia. Today, homosexual marriage would be as inconceivable as it was twenty years ago, if it were not for the influence of progressives on the culture and public education, and the decline of the influence of the church and conservatives espousing traditional values.

Progressives control the Democrat party and dominate the Republican party. President Obama advanced the homosexual civil rights movement and homosexual marriage so far, so quickly, in so many ways, it was difficult to keep up with half of what he did.

So we have this Supreme Court decision to legalize homosexual marriage for the country. Why must we respond?

(2.1) WHY? WE ARE REQUIRED TO DO SO.

The recognition of homosexual marriage has removed the last of any stigma against engaging in homosexual sexual behavior. Homosexual behavior is clearly defined as sin in the Bible. It is something no culture or nation has an interest in encouraging—indeed, they have every interest in discouraging it. So it should be stigmatized. It should be stigmatized just as stealing, adultery, or murder should be stigmatized. For centuries, engaging in homosexual behavior was stigmatized under law just as other behaviors were discouraged by law.

Homosexuals decided there was nothing wrong with their sexual behavior, so they began pressuring the American Psychiatric Association in 1970; and by 1973 the APA had removed homosexuality from the list of mental disorders in its official publication, the *Diagnostic and Statistical Manual of Psychiatric Disorders*, the DSM.[1] Homosexuals, not science, determined there was nothing wrong with homosexuals.

In the 2003 *Lawrence v. Texas* opinion, the Court struck down all remaining state laws against sodomy in the United States, sanctioning homosexual behavior by law. The Court declared people have a constitutional right to engage in homosexual behavior, so of course that is something which should not be stigmatized.

With *Obergefell*, the Court openly and brashly encourages people to engage in homosexual behavior. It does so under the guise of equality or marriage equality, as a high point in what we are to understand as just another American civil rights movement. And yet, man having sex with a man, or woman with a woman, is described as detestable in Leviticus 20:13, "If a man lies with a man as one lies with a woman, both of them have done what is detestable. They must be put to death; their blood will be on their own heads."

In 1 Corinthians 6:9–10 we read that homosexuals, along with a list of other sinners, will not enter into heaven, "Do you not know that the wicked will not inherit the kingdom of God? Do not be deceived: Neither the sexually immoral nor idolaters nor adulterers nor male prostitutes nor homosexual offenders nor thieves nor the greedy nor drunkards nor slanderers nor swindlers will inherit the kingdom of God."

Leviticus is Old Testament, before Christ. We understand from Leviticus that homosexuality is detestable, it is a sin, not that we are to put homosexuals to death. The death sentence is an indicator of how strongly God disapproves of homosexual behavior.

First Corinthians is New Testament, with Christ. And so we understand as we continue into 1 Corinthians 6:11 that homosexuals, like all sinners, can enter into heaven through Christ, "And that is what some of you were. But you were washed, you were sanctified, you were justified in the name of the Lord Jesus Christ and by the Spirit of our God."

Just as we are clearly told in the Bible that homosexual behavior is a sin, inarguably in these verses as well as in others; so we are also told what we are to do when faced with sin:

- *When I say to a wicked man, 'You will surely die,' and you do not warn him or speak out to dissuade him from his evil ways in order to save his life, that wicked man will die for his sin, and I will hold you accountable for his blood (Ezekiel 3:18).*

- *Have nothing to do with the fruitless deeds of darkness, but rather expose them (Ephesians 5:11).*

- *Anyone, then, who knows the good he ought to do and doesn't do it, sins (James 4:17).*

- *My brothers, if one of you should wander from the truth and someone should bring him back, remember this: Whoever turns a sinner from the error of his way will save him from death and cover over a multitude of sins (James 5:19-20).*

You cannot claim to love your neighbor if you encourage him or her to sin.

Christians must respond when everyone else in the culture is encouraging homosexual behavior. We are required to do so.

(2.2) WHY? ENFORCEMENT PROHIBITS SPREADING THE GOSPEL.

Secondly, Christians must respond to the enforcement of homosexual marriage because it is moving us quickly to the day when it is illegal, punishable under law, to proclaim the gospel of Christ in America.

Black Americans and women were denied rights which were recognized by law after their civil rights movements. The law provides penalties for violating those civil rights. Engaging in homosexual sexual behavior, and homosexual marriage, are civil rights according to the Court. The law must provide penalties for violating those civil rights as well.

Achieving one of the ends of the homosexual civil rights movement, the recognition of homosexual marriage, has the effect of justifying the means used to arrive at that end in our progressive culture. Homosexual marriage gives credibility to the homosexual civil rights movement, accusations of discrimination against homosexuals, and homophobia nonsense.

We had a black civil rights movement because of racism; we had a women's civil rights movement because of sexism; and we had a homosexual civil rights movement because of homophobia or so we were told.

Employees are trained in many workplaces today to correct their racist, sexist, or homophobic attitudes or beliefs. People are fired for racist, sexist, or homophobic speech.

We should not have allowed the homosexual civil rights movement to latch on to the black and women's civil rights movements to gain the kind of legitimacy it has. This was a civil rights movement for a *behavior*. It was not a civil rights movement for a group of people with immutable or unchangeable characteristics like their skin color, the racial group they were born into, or their sex. This was a civil rights movement for a group of people who want to engage in perverse and abnormal sexual behavior. Engaging in this behavior became a civil right.

Homosexual *identity* was thrown in, and this became a civil rights movement for people who wanted to identify themselves as homosexual. For decades homosexuals engaged in "coming out" as it was called, identifying themselves as homosexual, demanding acceptance for homosexuals and for their sexual behavior. Identifying or defining yourself as you see fit became a civil right.

Homosexuals who want to identify themselves as homosexual and engage in homosexual behavior have civil rights to do so we were told. To say homosexuals are sinners, and homosexual behavior is a sin, is to be in conflict with these civil rights. These are civil rights, and if you violate these civil rights you will be subject to penalties and punishment.

If the message of the gospel is we are all sinners, some of the behaviors we engage in are sins, and we need Christ and what He did for us on the cross; and if talking about sinners or sin is violating someone's civil rights, then you cannot freely speak about the gospel.

Accusations of violating someone's civil rights by describing their behavior as sin may not silence all Christians who want to spread the gospel. But you can be accused of more serious criminal offenses if you describe as sin a behavior someone has a civil right to engage in.

The Civil Rights Act of 1968 enabled federal prosecution of people who committed crimes against others because of the victim's race, color, religion, sex or national origin. In 2009, the *Matthew Shepard and James Byrd, Jr. Hate Crimes Prevention Act* became law. Matthew Shepard was a homosexual and James Byrd, Jr. was a black man. This law expanded the list of crimes committed against people to add their actual or perceived gender, sexual orientation, gender identity, or disability. Black Americans were already protected under the earlier federal law.

Before 2009, if a white man murdered a black man, he could be punished for murder. After the 2009 law, a white man who committed the same crime could be punished for murder and punished for committing a hate crime if he also chose his victim because he was black, that is to say if bias or racism also entered into the murder.

If you commit a crime against someone who is a member of a group which is protected under law, that carries an additional penalty. One could argue the classification of hate crime is unconstitutional, because it doesn't provide for equal treatment under the law. But we moved quickly past the time when we could question whether hate crime laws were constitutional. Anyone who questioned the hate crime classification in the beginning was immediately attacked by homosexual activists and progressives who declared that only someone who was racist, sexist, or some thing or other could possibly take issue with hate crime laws.

So today many would accuse me of engaging in hate speech when I question the constitutionality of hate crime legislation.

The classification of hate crime led to the recognition of hate speech. And this classification of speech was contrived so it could be argued that hate speech encourages or leads to hate crimes, and therefore hate speech should be illegal. You should be penalized and punished under law for hate speech.

While it was argued that hate crime legislation would not conflict with First Amendment rights, hate crime led to hate speech. And while hate speech was not said to be illegal when it was introduced, this progressive classification has led to bans on hate speech in universities and schools across the country. Hate speech, as some of the so-called victims who are exposed to it define it, is increasingly banned, and people are punished and penalized for engaging in hate speech even when it is not against any law. Increasing efforts to ban hate speech are leading to laws against hate speech.

So in the *Pew Research Center's Spring 2015 Global Attitudes Survey*, when asked if people should be allowed to make public statements offensive to minorities, forty percent of Americans ages 18–34 thought the government should be able to prevent people making such statements.[2]

Forty percent of these people think government should prevent offensive speech. The gospel of Christ is particularly offensive to homosexuals who do not want to hear there is anything wrong with their sexual behavior. How does the government prevent such offensive speech? By making it illegal.

The irony here is these people went through government school progressive indoctrination under teachers who, in days past, demanded and defended anything and everything as free speech—Nazis marching in Skokie, Illinois, fools burning the American flag, and the like.

You are in conflict with homosexual civil rights if you say homosexual behavior is a sin. You are labeled homophobic if you say homosexual behavior is a sin. In fact, if you say there is anything wrong with homosexuality or homosexual behavior then you are homophobic. If you don't celebrate homosexual marriage, you are homophobic. If you think there is any reason it might be better for a child to be raised by a father with a mother, you are homophobic. You might think heterosexual men should not be put into Girl Scout leadership positions to take girls camping in the woods because they might sexually abuse them; but if you think homosexual men should not be put into Boy Scout leadership positions to take boys camping in the woods, you are homophobic. The list of things you might think or say which indicate you are homophobic is ever expanding, as the penalties and punishments for homophobia become harsher.

Any so-called "homophobic" speech is labeled hate speech. You are said to be engaging in hate speech if you tell someone homosexual behavior is a sin. You are said to be encouraging hate crimes against homosexuals when you say homosexual behavior is a sin. While homosexual activists may argue it should be illegal for someone to say homosexual behavior is a sin; progressives think the world would be a much better place if it were illegal for Christians to say any behavior is a sin, and that is where they are determined to bring us.

Classifying talk of sin as hate speech, and punishing people for engaging in hate speech, or making hate speech illegal, effectively prevents delivery of half the gospel message. If you cannot talk about sin, you might, sort of, continue to talk about Christ. So progressives introduced us to Homophobia's idiot cousin, Islamophobia.

Like homophobia, you are Islamophobic if you believe there is anything wrong with the false religion of Islam. The list of things you might think or say which would indicate you are Islamophobic is ever expanding, as the penalties and punishments for Islamophobia become harsher. If you cannot say Islam is a false religion, and Christ is the only way, then you cannot deliver the other half of the gospel message. If you cannot speak of sin, and cannot say Christ is the only way, you cannot proclaim the gospel.

Whether or not progressives intended homosexual marriage as a means of silencing Christians in this country does not matter; that has been the effect of their influence and their stupid ideas on public policy.

Christians must respond to homosexual marriage because we are required to do so. It is our task to acknowledge sin. To go along with homosexual marriage is to encourage people to sin.

Christians must respond to homosexual marriage because our function is to spread the gospel. The enforcement of homosexual marriage will prohibit that.

CHAPTER 3

HOW MUST CHRISTIANS RESPOND TO HOMOSEXUAL "MARRIAGE"?

So if you agree we must respond, how, then, should Christians respond?

When told we must go along with homosexual marriage, as a consequence of this Supreme Court decision, the Christian response must be, "No!"

When told we must go along with homosexual marriage because to refuse is to break the law, the Christian response must be, "This is not a matter of law. An opinion of the Supreme Court is not law."

Christians do not encourage others to sin. Christians must have regard for law, the rule of law, and this constitutional republic we have been so blessed to live under. Christians do not seek to break laws, undermine the rule of law, or violate the Constitution, the law of the land, which is what those who would enforce this Court decision as law are doing. Enforcing this Supreme Court opinion is not law, it is lawlessness. Enforcing this Supreme Court opinion is not law, it is rule.

The day after the opinion was announced, family organizations across the country sent out emails asking for donations to support upcoming legal battles. Within a few days after the opinion, many churches responded by rewriting their bylaws to indicate they would not perform homosexual marriages. They began revising their rules about the public use of church facilities, changing policies so they might not be accused of discrimination. They sought legal advice from lawyers and insurers to protect themselves.

Some churches began to consider not performing any marriages at all, rather than face the consequences for refusing to perform homosexual marriages. Those outside the church increased calls for the church, the government, or both to "get out of the marriage business" altogether.

The argument that churches should not have, or should give up, tax exemptions was revitalized, anticipating the federal government will hold those exemptions over our heads to force churches to recognize homosexual marriages.

Then there was the response of the Kentucky county clerk, Kim Davis, the first response to the Court opinion receiving significant national attention. Davis stopped issuing marriage licenses after the Court opinion and she eventually spent five days in jail. At the end of 2015, the governor of Kentucky issued an executive order to change the marriage license form so county clerks' names were no longer included on it.

These are the primary responses to *Obergefell* thus far, and these responses have been wrong, wrong, wrong!

In choosing to fund and prepare for upcoming legal battles, we are affirming this Supreme Court opinion is law, and we are conceding homosexual marriage. We do not and will not have the time for legal battles to roll back homosexual marriage if it is accepted as the "law of the land." Tens of thousands of young people will be encouraged to engage in homosexual behavior in the next few years. Since the Court opinion, activists have redoubled their efforts to normalize homosexuality and now gender nonconformity in government schools.

Exceptions were allowed when abortion was legalized. Doctors and nurses who did not want to perform abortions were allowed to keep the blood off their hands. While there were such exceptions, there was time for legal battles and other action. But the exceptions for being involved with abortion have been or are being eliminated. Likewise, if any exceptions for homosexual marriage are allowed, they will be eliminated. There will be no exceptions giving us the time for legal battles or rolling back homosexual marriage.

The concerns of the gullible may have been relieved by Justice Anthony Kennedy when he declared in *Obergefell* that:

> *[R]eligions, and those who adhere to religious doctrines, may continue to advocate with utmost, sincere*

conviction that, by divine precepts, same-sex marriage should not be condoned. The First Amendment ensures that religious organizations and persons are given proper protection as they seek to teach the principles that are so fulfilling and so central to their lives and faiths, and to their own deep aspirations to continue the family structure they have long revered.

This was meaningless blather. Kennedy implied there would be some kind of exception for religious groups and persons. Well, as this law which isn't a law was applied immediately after the Court opinion, no one in any sort of elected or government position like the Kentucky county clerk would be allowed to refuse to condone homosexual marriage. Christians and religious business owners must provide services for homosexual marriages if they provide them for real marriages.

Again, there will be no exceptions and there will be no time for legal battles over this.

Churches seeking to protect themselves are likewise only affirming this Court opinion is law, and are conceding homosexual marriage. It is simple cowardice which leads many to allow themselves to be silenced.

In retreating and attempting to draw some kind of line just outside the church door, saying only that we will not perform homosexual marriages here, churches are doing just what progressives would have them do: giving up culture, law, and government to be entirely directed by progressives. They are doing what people in churches did in early Nazi Germany.

And let's just give up any tax exemptions churches may claim, so more money can go to the federal government to spend rather than churches. Let's send more of our money to the federal government to provide funding for Planned Parenthood to harvest body parts from babies, and let's send more of our money to the federal government to give billions more to Iran to murder Jews. I don't think so.

Grown-ups don't have to spend much more time than that to consider the arguments about the government or church getting out of the marriage business altogether either. The government has an interest in encouraging marriage and families as the only means of producing a next generation of emotionally healthy children to become citizens. Progressives would like nothing more than for the church to entirely hand over marriage to the government to redefine family and parenthood, to eliminate any role for fathers, to change marriage to an entirely government-enforced contractual agreement, to license people to have children—on and on the lunatic list of progressive changes we must make to marriage will go.

What most Christians have taken away from the story of the Kentucky county clerk appears to have been wrong as well. Davis was released from jail, not because of protests about religious liberty, not because it was recognized anyone might be allowed to refuse to be involved in homosexual marriages, but because it was confirmed others in the office would continue to issue marriage licenses for homosexual couples—in effect the "law" would be enforced.

In the minds of most Americans, Davis refused to sign marriage licenses because homosexual marriage is against her religious beliefs. But that was not enough, was it? She was not allowed to refuse because of her religious beliefs. She would likely still be in jail if others in that county office had not agreed to issue the licenses.

In removing the county clerks' names from the marriage licenses so Christians are not forced to go along with homosexual marriages, Kentucky only affirmed the Court opinion is law, and conceded homosexual marriage for the rest of the country.

If we argue that we will not go along with homosexual marriage because it is against our Christian beliefs, we lose. There will be consequences, including loss of jobs and careers, and time in jail. If this is our only response, if we remain silent until we are forced to argue this, we will be conceding and affirming for the rest of the country that there is a law here that applies in the first place.

We are affirming there is a law when we explain we cannot obey it because of our Christian beliefs. We are affirming a SCOTUS opinion is the law of the land as our progressive betters tell us. We should not be in, we are *not* in, the position of refusing to go along with a law.

There are consequences for us in losing the argument that we will not go along with homosexual marriage because of our Christian beliefs. But the consequences for not declaring that it is wrong to accept that there is some law here in the first place will be much worse.

In addition to taking a stand as Christians, we have to take a stand as Americans. We have to stand for the law, the rule of law, and this Constitution we are all so blessed to live under. We have to oppose the enforcement of this SCOTUS opinion as law.

It will not work to do this as individuals. We have to compel our elected officials to do their jobs, to enforce our state's marriage laws. Most states do not recognize homosexual marriage under state law. It is wrong for a federal law to override the state laws which have always regulated marriage in this country, and there is no federal law as a result of this Court opinion anyway. Some elected state officials may not refuse to enforce the Court opinion because they have Christian beliefs which lead them to consider it unjust or immoral. But they should have enough sense to recognize how enforcing an opinion of the Supreme Court as a law undermines the Constitution. If they don't, they shouldn't be in the offices they are holding. They should recognize their function is to enforce the will of the people, not the will of our progressive elites.

CHAPTER 4

WHAT FOLLOWS IF CHRISTIANS DO NOT RESPOND TO HOMOSEXUAL "MARRIAGE"?

If we do not say "No!" to what progressives are doing to marriage, if we will not say something about even this, then progressives will not be opposed with any success on anything else they are doing.

What else are progressives doing? If they are allowed to continue to direct public policy in this country, what else will follow? I will focus on two things here, and in doing so I am not making any predictions about the future. What I am describing has largely already happened or been done. The first is the Gender Identity Movement. The second is our continuing, uninterrupted descent into world government.

(4.1) WHAT FOLLOWS? THE GENDER IDENTITY MOVEMENT.

Consider the progression, or regression if you will, described in Romans 1: 21–29:

For although they knew God, they neither glorified him as God nor gave thanks to him, but their thinking became futile and their foolish hearts were darkened. Although they claimed to be wise, they became fools and exchanged the glory of the immortal God for images made to look like mortal man and birds and animals and reptiles.

Therefore God gave them over in the sinful desires of their hearts to sexual impurity for the degrading of their bodies with one another. They exchanged the truth of God for a lie, and worshiped and served created things rather than the Creator—who is forever praised. Amen.

Because of this, God gave them over to shameful lusts. Even their women exchanged natural relations for unnatural ones. In the same way the men also abandoned natural relations with women and were inflamed with lust for one another. Men committed indecent acts with other men, and received in themselves the due penalty for their perversion.

Furthermore, since they did not think it worthwhile to retain the knowledge of God, he gave them over to a depraved mind, to do what ought not to be done.

Here we read about futile thinking and foolish people who know of God but choose to worship other things. God gives them over to their sinful desires, letting them have their way, and to "sexual impurity for the degrading of their bodies," and to "shameful lusts," including homosexual relations. Finally, when in their minds they no longer think of God and what He would have them do, He abandons them, and their minds become depraved and they do all manner of things they should not do.

The passage speaks of a giving over by God which leads to homosexual relations, and a further giving over which leads to other things which should not be done. People go from doing sinful and stupid things to ever more sinful and stupid things. They determine the knowledge of God is not worthwhile; so they have no fear of God which, as the Bible tells us, is the beginning of all wisdom. They are short on knowledge and wisdom and long on sin and stupidity.

So in America we are going from this homosexual identity movement, which sanctioned and encouraged homosexual behavior under the guise of a civil rights movement, to the gender identity civil rights movement. This gender identity movement is insane, spiritually evil, and stupid. It is a product of depraved minds.

America declared to the world with homosexual marriage that there is no God who created us male and female. That is what we declared to the world. We were not created male and female, for each other, to be united as one in marriage, as we read in the Bible. Now we go a step further with this gender identity madness, and America is declaring to the world that there is no God who created us. That is what we declare to the world. We are not male or female as made by a creator. We were assigned our genders after we were born, by doctors who were sometimes mistaken in thinking those of us they circumcised were boys.

Homosexuality is rebellion against God, and gender denial simply takes that rebellion a step further.

We used to understand a person's sex was biological, either male or female, and their gender was boy or girl, man or woman. A person's gender identity was how they identified themselves. A boy identified as a boy, and a girl knew she was a girl. Sometimes, for whatever reason, there was disagreement between a person's biological sex and their gender identity, and these people were considered transgender.

The American Psychiatric Association used to refer to Gender Identity Disorder in its *Diagnostic and Statistical Manual of Mental Disorders*, the DSM. Gender Identity Disorder was changed to the more politically correct Gender Dysphoria in 2013, as the APA decided gender nonconformity is not a mental disorder. Apparently there's nothing wrong with a boy who thinks he's a girl, so they decided referring to this as a disorder was too stigmatizing.[1]

As I described earlier, the APA removed homosexuality from the list of mental disorders in the DSM in 1973 to appease homosexuals who wanted to identify themselves as homosexual. During the homosexual civil rights movement, it was argued over and over again, up to and including in the amicus briefs sent to the Supreme Court for the *Obergefell* hearing, that there is nothing wrong with homosexuality, because it is no longer considered a disorder by the APA. They had removed it from the DSM.

One has to wonder how long it will take for the American Psychiatric Association to declare stark raving madness is not a mental disorder.

So we had the homosexual identity civil rights movement, and now we have the gender identity civil rights movement for people who can no longer be said to suffer from a disorder. There is an ever-expanding list of gender identities you can choose from, and people of every gender identity are entitled to protections and civil rights just as homosexuals were. Gender identity is as valid as homosexual identity, and worthy of acknowledgment, encouragement, and civil rights advancement under law.

There are people who are *agender* or *androgynous*, with both female and male gender identities. There are people who are *bigender*, and people who are *gender fluid*, who may feel like a man on Monday and a woman on Wednesday. There are people who are *genderqueer* or *non-binary*, who are outside of the conventional and traditional male and female system, and challenge what they regard as its restrictive and unhealthy norms. There are people who are *pangender* or all genders, the real saints of inclusiveness who are so accepting of the ever-widening diversity of genders.

On and on the list goes. There is a whole new vocabulary for this civil rights movement, and all the kids in government schools are to be taught about this important civil rights movement which followed the homosexual civil rights movement which followed the women's and black civil rights movements in America.

So we will encourage people to change their genders as they wish. We will encourage people to surgically remove or chemically alter parts of their bodies, encourage them to maim themselves, in efforts to change their biological sex.

We did not say "No!" to any aspect of this homosexual civil rights movement, so we cannot logically say "No!" to this gender identity civil rights movement. To do so is to discriminate and to be a bigot. Those who would deny a boy the right to identify himself as a girl (or a cat or a dolphin), or tell a boy he cannot use the girls' bathroom or shower with the girls in a government school, who accuse others of discriminating against homosexuals or being bigots because they don't want to be involved in a homosexual marriage, are the worst kind of hypocrites.

This gender identity movement could not have happened without the successful homosexual identity movement capped off with homosexual marriage. It followed inevitably behind. People have been working at this gender identity movement for years, but it didn't explode until immediately after the homosexual marriage opinion was announced, and it was declared as accepted as law by Americans, whether they accepted it or not.

This gender identity movement is a consequence of the progressive homosexual civil rights movement.

Immediately after the SCOTUS opinion on marriage, the indoctrination about and enforcement of homosexual civil rights went into overdrive in government schools in the fall of 2015. And in government schools, boys and girls who thought they were another gender began to demand their civil rights. Actually, it wasn't the boys or girls as much as it was their crazy parents or school officials.

Because no one said "No!" to the SCOTUS opinion on homosexual marriage, we should expect to see an opinion on gender identity soon. By June 2016, one year after *Obergefell*, seventeen states had passed legislation requiring that people be allowed to use the bathroom of the gender they identify with. Eleven State Attorneys General had also filed a lawsuit in response to the Obama administration's directive that schools should allow students to use the bathroom of the gender they identify with, or risk the loss of federal funding.

As a result of these state laws and/or the lawsuit, this gender identity civil rights issue will quickly be taken to the Supreme Court. And the Court will issue another opinion as law, just as they did with *Obergefell*, directing us to allow everyone to use the bathroom of the gender they identify with.

Americans were slowly and methodically forced to accept homosexual civil rights and marriage. The acceptance of what the APA yesterday termed Gender Identity Disorder has been quicker and more brutally enforced.

In April 2015, Bruce Jenner came out as what he described as a woman. It was amusing to watch at first as gender identity political correctness was enforced among the talking heads in news and entertainment media. Early on some commentators continued to call Bruce Jenner "Bruce" rather than "Caitlan," and they were set upon immediately by their politically correct progressive peers.

It is distressing to consider how this regression in Romans chapter 1 from people being turned over by God to have their way and then to degrade their bodies, to go from foolish and futile thinking to depraved minds, has been played out as Americans have moved from the homosexual to gender identity civil rights movements.

Understand that we are to go along with this gender identity movement just as we went along with this homosexual identity movement. You will celebrate homosexual marriages, and you will allow boys to share the bathroom and shower with your daughters if you send them to a government school, whether you like it or not. You will encourage homosexuals and people who suffer a Gender Identity Disorder to destroy themselves, or you will keep your mouth shut.

The progressive, homosexual civil rights movement champions opened the door to this gender identity madness. Pandora's box was opened and only God can close it now.

(4.2) WHAT FOLLOWS? WORLD GOVERNMENT.

Among followers of Christ there are several different schools of thought about the rise of the Antichrist described in the Bible. Some think this is an organization or system already in place influencing the world. Others expect to see a world dictator in the final days. Most people understand that we are otherwise moving toward world government or *global governance* as some now term it. Leadership behind the climate change movement wants a world government to deal with climate, and a tax on all nations to fund that government. World government will inevitably become totalitarian rule, no matter how many academic and intellectual fools insist they could do it better than the last dictator or group of elites who tried.

But I think everyone with different views on a world dictator or government can agree on one thing: America will have to go before a global dictator comes into power or we have a world government. America is potentially the only obstacle to world government or totalitarian rule and dictatorship.

We declared we would not be ruled by tyrants, and fought the Revolutionary War to free ourselves. We created a Constitution so we could rule ourselves, so we could live under the rule of law and not the rule of men.

According to some, hundreds of thousands of Americans died in our Civil War to free black slaves so they would no longer be owned by other men. In truth, more died in that conflict over states and rule by federal government, than died defending the institution of slavery. But in both versions of the Civil War, Americans fought against being ruled by others.

Many, many Americans bled out their lives defending and protecting this country and you, and the world, from totalitarian rule under Nazism, communism and now Islam.

America has been the best and most hoped for model of limited rule by government. So if the world is to have one government, a dictator or totalitarian rule; America, our Constitution, and our constitutional republic will have to go first.

What does this have to do with homosexual marriage, with *Obergefell*?

This has everything to do with that SCOTUS opinion.

When historians write about the fall of nations and civilizations like Rome, for example, they usually have a list of broad factors which contributed to the decline, and a detailed list of historical events. Rome fell because of corrupt government, economic decline, an overextended military, and barbarian invasions, among other broad factors. And we have a detailed history of the specific barbarian invasions that happened.

Interestingly, grown-ups in America know that our nation is in decline; and, like Rome, we have corrupt government, economic decline (which will soon become collapse), we have an overextended (and underfunded) military, and we are having our own barbarian invasion.

Future historians of America would write about our constitutional republic form of government. We were born as a nation as a constitutional republic. If they wrote about our nation's decline and fall, the broad factors which contributed would include those things which impacted on our constitutional republic form of government. And the *Obergefell* opinion delivered in June 2015, would be on the top of every historian's detailed list of historical events. That opinion was a pivotal, critical victory for people who want to end our constitutional republic form of government; people who want us to discard the American Constitution.

If everyone agrees, if no one can be bothered to say anything, when five unelected lawyers on the Supreme Court give us their opinion and tell us that is the law, then we are done with this Constitution and we are done with this constitutional republic.

If we do not respond, if instead we agree we are done with this Constitution and this republic, there will be no other chance to effectively respond in the future. I have a hope that we have just enough of a remnant left, there are just enough grown-ups in America who might yet respond to this Court opinion. We may have just enough veterans left, enough grandparents and people with children, enough of those people who still go out to Memorial Day parades in small communities and stand up when people walk past with our flag, enough people who understand it is wrong to take our liberties and freedom and this

Constitution for granted, and what an offense to God this surely must be, to respond. We may have just enough people left to draw and hold a line today. Tomorrow we will not.

We may just be at that 52 percent the people in Britain were at when they voted to leave the European Union in June 2016. While there was much debate about the reasons for voting for or against Brexit, our cousins across the pond were in effect voting on whether or not the world should continue to have a Britain. And just fifty-two percent voted it should.

If Americans will not respond, if we are done with this Constitution and this republic, then understand this: the Constitution is the only thing that separates us from them. By "them" I mean those people who live in other countries where agents of the state can take you out from your home in the middle of the night, where you can be tortured and put to death for speaking out against your rulers or your government; other countries where people do not get a trial by a jury of their peers, or where they get no trial at all; other countries where people are persecuted for practicing a religion which is not sanctioned by the state.

If we are done with this Constitution and this republic, it will be much easier to bring America into a global Islamic state. It will be easier to implement sharia law in America, because the American Constitution is the only obstacle to the implementation of sharia law in America.

Understand this: under sharia law, everyone reading this book would likely be subject to rape, enslavement, and particularly savage and brutal murder. You would likely be forced to watch as these things were done to your children and grandchildren before they were done to you. That includes any Muslim readers as well, who are not part of the same group or sect as the ones holding the butcher knives.

So there's a lot at stake here.

Everything is at stake here.

CHAPTER 5

WHY MUST ALL AMERICANS RESPOND TO HOMOSEXUAL "MARRIAGE"?

If you're an American who is not a Christian and you've read this far, you're probably expecting me to continue on a long rant about homosexual marriage and the SCOTUS decision which "made it legal."

After a point, I don't care whether you are for or against homosexual marriage. As a Christian, I am fundamentally opposed to it. I don't care whether you are a Democrat or Republican either. I detest both political parties.

I don't have much to say about the subject of the decision, homosexual marriage, which you might expect me to go on at length about in a book with this title.

About the subject, I would simply say that homosexual marriage encourages homosexual behavior; that is to say it encourages some men to have what they describe as sex with other men, and women with women. If homosexual marriage is a good thing, then it follows that men having what they describe as sex with other men, and women with women, is a good thing.

Anyone who can read a Bible understands this behavior is a sin. As a Christian, I don't encourage other people to sin; therefore, I oppose homosexual marriage. That is a real no-brainer for me.

The Court declared homosexual marriage is the same as heterosexual marriage; that we are to place the same value on both. But the sexual activity people engage in as part of a heterosexual marriage is required to produce babies, while the sexual activity people engage in as part of a homosexual marriage can never produce babies, and leads to much higher incidences of HIV transmission and a host of other diseases.

To survive, our nation has every interest in continuing to encourage heterosexual marriage. We have no reason or interest whatsoever in encouraging homosexual marriage. So again, opposing homosexual marriage is a real no-brainer for me.

But let's look past the subject of the decision, homosexual marriage, and consider a few other things about that particular SCOTUS opinion, because the opinion was about much more than homosexuals and marriage.

(5.1) THE HEIGHTS OF ABUSE

In the final weeks before the decision was announced, everyone was guessing what it would be. The Democrats and Republicans wanted the Court to legalize homosexual marriage because they thought it should be legal, or they just wanted a decision, any decision, so they could declare the issue was settled and it wouldn't become a topic in the presidential campaign, as it did not. So when they reported on the Court's opinion, the liars and deceivers in the media declared homosexual marriage was "the law of the land."

I think I'm the only person I knew at the time who was wondering, "Who cares what the Supreme Court opinion on homosexual marriage is?" The Supreme Court does not tell us in a constitutional republic what the law is on marriage or homosexual marriage. It is the function of our legislators, our elected representatives in a constitutional republic, to tell us what the law is; and particularly our elected state legislators in this constitutional republic.

Since the 1803 *Marbury v. Madison* decision, under which the Supreme Court gave itself judicial review authority, by which it could declare laws enacted by our elected representatives are unconstitutional and invalid, the Court has taken to making laws as well.

So 212 years later, the Supreme Court reached the high point in its abuse of constitutional authority when it allegedly "legalized" homosexual marriage, when it said the Constitution requires homosexual marriage. A decision by the Court, or an opinion of the Court as it is also referred to, is not law. A Supreme Court decision or opinion is called a decision or opinion because it is not a law. If it was a law, we could just describe it as such and we wouldn't have to consider whether to refer to it as a decision or an opinion.

We began a civil war in 1861 because of conflicts over states' rights, tariffs, and several other things including slavery. Prior to the Civil War, government for most Americans was state government. Confederate states called their citizens to war, as the Union states did. Southerners responded to Northern aggression and defended their homes. The Civil War ended in 1865.

So 150 years later, the Supreme Court reached the high point in its abuse of constitutional authority when it legalized homosexual marriage, when it declared all state laws which didn't provide for homosexual marriage were unconstitutional. This was the high point in the federal government taking for itself any and all powers reserved to the states by the Constitution.

Marriage has always been regulated by state legislatures. Before *Obergefell*, twelve state legislatures had enacted laws that allowed for homosexual marriage. Before the opinion, thirty-seven states allowed homosexual marriage by court decisions; and one state, Maine, allowed it because of a ballot initiative.[1]

Elected representatives had followed the constitutional process and enacted marriage laws the people wanted to live under in those twelve states, as well as in the other thirty-eight. The courts decided what marriage law was to be in thirty-seven states, and then the Supreme Court decided what marriage is to be in all fifty states.

The Supreme Court does not have the authority under the Constitution to tell us what the law is or is not.

(5.2) IT'S UNCONSTITUTIONAL

Laws are said to be constitutional or unconstitutional.

The Supreme Court gave itself judicial review authority, by which nine oligarchs could declare laws created by our elected representatives were unconstitutional and invalid. A group of nine, or rather just five out of nine, could decide what is or is not law.

An *oligarch* is a fancy word for a member of a group of dictators. We rarely refer to the plural of *dictator*, because the term nearly always refers to one person. The whole point of being a dictator is to be the only one. So it makes more sense to refer to these nine members of the Court as oligarchs.

So, not long after the Constitution was delivered, the judicial branch began judging whether laws were constitutional.

The Constitution is the law of the land. Laws enacted through our government established by the Constitution must agree with the Constitution. Laws cannot violate the rights we are declared to have in the Declaration of Independence or the protections and rights given to us by the Constitution. We have a Bill of Rights, with an enumerated list of fundamental and foundational rights, like freedom of speech, for example. Any law which violates or denies freedom of speech is in conflict with the Constitution and is not a law.

Laws have to be in agreement with the Constitution. Apparently the authors expected the legislative branch would not create laws which were not in agreement. The founders would never have given the judicial branch the authority to declare whether or not a law enacted by our elected representatives is a law. The function of the judicial branch is to work with the laws they are given by the legislative branch.

The founders did not include among the checks and balances in the Constitution an additional check upon the legislative branch to confirm its laws were constitutional. They expected laws enacted by the legislative branch would be so.

They anticipated their posterity would follow and apply the Constitution they had given us. They did not anticipate how lazy and apathetic Americans would become. They did not anticipate how many Americans would take everything they had been blessed with as Americans for granted. They did not anticipate their posterity actively undermining and destroying the Constitution.

The founders didn't think we needed that additional check. Some of them also didn't think we needed a bill of rights. Indeed, Alexander Hamilton argued in Federalist No. 84 that bills of rights were unnecessary when he wrote:

They would contain various exceptions to powers not granted . . . For why declare that things shall not be

*done which there is no power to do? Why, for instance,
should it be said that the liberty of the press shall not be
restrained, when no power is given by which restrictions
may be imposed?*

Our government, established by the Constitution, does not have the authority under the Constitution to restrict the freedom of the press, so why include freedom of the press in a bill of rights? Why include freedom of religion or freedom of speech in a bill of rights when the government does not have the authority to deny those rights? Why include a right to bear arms when the government does not have the authority to deny your right to bear arms?

Our founders thought, and hoped, we would follow the Constitution they had given us. If we had, there would have been no need for our Bill of Rights; or for an additional check on the constitutionality of laws enacted by the legislative branch.

But I thank God they also gave us our Bill of Rights. Without our Bill of Rights, this constitutional republic would have ended long ago.

It was expected we would follow the Constitution, and therefore the greatest part of the laws we would agree to live our lives under would be enacted by our state, and not federal government, as well. An unconstitutional law enacted by state legislators can and will more readily be repealed by the citizens of that state who are able to get the attention of their elected representatives and replace them if needed.

Those who make law under our Constitution are elected. When they make bad law, they can be replaced. Members of the judicial branch are not elected under our Constitution because it is not their function to make law.

The founders did not anticipate that Americans would agree so easily to being ruled again. Those with Hamilton must have expected their posterity would not allow the government they had been given to restrict or deny their freedoms of religion or speech and other freedoms if they were not enumerated in a bill of rights.

They also told us we had a right to change this government if we found ourselves and our children living under the rule of men rather than the rule of law. We have been living under the rule of men again for quite some time already. As I explain later in these pages, the executive branch has been issuing executive orders as law, and enforcing judicial branch opinions and federal agency rules and regulations as law for too long already to turn it back.

We have devolved to allowing someone other than our lawmakers to confirm the constitutionality of the laws they create, to decide whether they should be laws at all.

So let's consider then whether a law establishing homosexual marriage is constitutional in light of the First and Ninth Amendments.

About That First Amendment

The First Amendment of the Constitution reads, "Congress shall make no law respecting an establishment of religion, or prohibiting the free exercise thereof; or abridging the freedom of speech or of the press; or the right of the people peaceably to assemble, and to petition the Government for a redress of grievances."

Article 1, Section 1, gave legislative powers to Congress. The executive and judicial branches were given no legislative powers by the Constitution.

We can paraphrase and shorten the text and keep it's meaning to focus on two parts here: Congress shall not make a law prohibiting the free exercise of religion, and Congress shall not make a law abridging the freedom of speech.

Under the Constitution, we have freedom of religion and freedom of speech, and Congress cannot make any law which makes it unlawful for us to exercise those freedoms or takes those freedoms from us.

A federal law which prohibited or abridged those freedoms would have to come from Congress. By definition, it would not be a law if it came from the executive or judicial branches of the federal government.

It was a branch of the federal government, the Supreme Court of the judicial branch, and not the Congress or legislative branch, which made homosexual marriage legal for the nation.

About That Ninth Amendment

The Ninth Amendment reads: "The enumeration in the Constitution of certain rights shall not be construed to deny or disparage others retained by the people."

Forests have been leveled to produce the papers in piles and books on shelves holding the debates, discussions, and diatribes about the meaning and intent of the words in the Constitution. Much has been written to explain how the words do not mean what they say by people who would have us believe that you must be a constitutional scholar to understand our Constitution.

There is Ninth Amendment debate about rights which are enumerated and unenumerated in the Constitution, state and federal law, individual and collective rights, and so on.

A simple reading of the Ninth Amendment tells both the scholar and a commoner like me that the authors of the Constitution considered there were or could be some rights the people have which might be understood "to deny or disparage" other rights the people have; and those rights must not "deny or disparage" other rights.

The founders had reason to speak to a possible conflict between rights enumerated in the Constitution, like those specified in the Bill of Rights; and other rights like those inalienable rights we have which are not listed in the Bill of Rights. It was understood, however, that one right cannot be understood to "deny or disparage" another right.

The founders did not need to say much more, here again, because they thought we would follow and apply the Constitution they had given us. They did not anticipate that progressives and statists would be allowed to undermine the Constitution and do their dirty work to the extent they have.

Progressives hijacked our Constitution, and instead of using it to limit government, they used it to build up government. The Constitution limited government so it would not come into conflict with, or deny, our inalienable and enumerated rights. Progressives declared our rights come from government (we can forget about inalienable rights coming from God which cannot be taken away by government) and they are hell-bent on concocting as many gutter-class rights as possible. Government gets bigger and more powerful with each right it grants, delivers upon, and defends.

Eventually, when you have an unlimited number of "rights," some will come into conflict with others.

So we had an inalienable right to life which came into conflict with a gutter-class right to an abortion, for example. See "About That Right to Choose" in the Appendix later.

The very people so determined to create as many rights as they could, as a means of building up government, decided a right to life must not be assigned to a baby before it is born. Sixty seconds before it is born, a baby does not have the right to life which it has sixty seconds later. The baby is alive before it is born. The baby is a baby before it is born. The only difference between a baby with a right to life which should be defended and one without that right, is the first baby is sixty seconds older than the other. What a difference a mere sixty seconds can make!

You would think that if extending as many rights to as many people as possible was an inherently good thing, progressives would want to include babies sixty seconds before they are born. The fact is, progressives don't want some of those babies to be born; they want them dead, especially the black ones. I explain that later in these pages.

About Both Those Amendments

So what do the First and Ninth Amendments have to say about homosexual marriage? They don't say anything.

The Constitution doesn't say anything about heterosexual marriage either. Heterosexuals don't have a constitutional right to marry. But five out of nine unelected lawyers on the Court decided homosexuals do. Heterosexuals don't have a constitutional right to marry. Why should homosexuals?

But if we must take this SCOTUS opinion seriously, if homosexuals really have a constitutional right to marry, then the First and Ninth Amendments do have something to say about homosexual marriage.

Let's play along with those progressives and their homosexual activist tools who managed to get a favorable decision on homosexual marriage from the Court. They couldn't get Congress to enact a law creating homosexual marriage, so they went to the Court for a decision to be enforced as a law.

Let's play along with all the media liars and deceivers aligned with those progressives, who declared on June 26, 2015, that "homosexual marriage is the law of the land."

Let's play along with the Supreme Court and try to take this opinion seriously. Forget that two of the justices had already been performing homosexual marriages before they gathered for the hearing and the long hours of debate, justices who didn't have the character or integrity to recuse themselves.

Let's not refer to this as a dirty opinion but rather as a decision. The members of the Court gave us their decision on homosexual marriage. They decided for us. They should make these decisions for us.

Let's play along with all those Democrat politicians who wanted the Court to give us the law on homosexual marriage so they could start in on their next five civil rights movements and all those Republican politicians who wanted the Court to tell us what the law is on homosexual marriage so they could say the issue was settled and they wouldn't have to talk about it ever again. We pay these louts to enact the laws we and our children have to live under, and they all take an oath to support and defend the Constitution of the United States, but let's play along with the politicians who deferred to the oligarchs on the Court to tell us what the law is.

So we have a "law" which says homosexuals have a right to marry.

Is this law constitutional?

Clearly not.

According to the First Amendment, there can be no laws prohibiting the free exercise of religion or abridging the freedom of speech. As this "law" which says homosexuals have a right to marry has been applied and enforced, it has done more to prohibit the free exercise of religion and abridge people's freedom of speech than it will ever do to make homosexuals happy.

According to the Ninth Amendment, a constitutional right to homosexual marriage cannot be understood to "deny or disparage" freedom of religion or freedom of speech. As this "law" which says homosexuals have a right to marry has been applied and enforced, it has done more to "deny or disparage" freedom of religion and speech than it will ever do to make homosexuals happy.

Americans, religious or not, who do not wish to provide a marriage-related service for homosexuals are to be fined and put out of business or put into jail. People who would say anything that indicates they don't want to celebrate a homosexual marriage are to be silenced.

This "law," which isn't a law because it didn't come from a legislative body, is unconstitutional because it clearly violates the First and Ninth Amendments.

(5.3) A CRITICAL VICTORY

Obergefell was a critical victory for people who want to end our constitutional republic. The victory was not the Court's opinion itself; it was the manner in which everyone went along with it.

It took decades to get us into the position where most Americans simply accept a SCOTUS opinion as law; decades of dumbing down in government schools where kids never even read the Constitution, decades where everyone has taken the Constitution for granted, decades of political "leaders" entirely disregarding the Constitution.

Today we have political candidates running for public offices who have never studied or likely even read the Constitution, including those running for the highest office in the land who take an oath of office, half of which is an oath to protect and defend the Constitution of the United States, who will enter office with no idea what that means or interest in doing it, and will undermine it from the first day in most everything they do.

Along the way to moving most Americans to accept a SCOTUS opinion as law, the Court pulled the same stunt in 1973 with the *Roe v. Wade* decision. Back then the Court declared state laws against abortion in twenty-seven states were unconstitutional, and declared abortion legal in all states. Many people did not accept this decision; it is still debated today; and states have enacted laws to reduce or limit the abortions which seven unelected lawyers on the Court declared legal in 1973.

The *Obergefell* homosexual marriage decision, however, has been more widely accepted as law. Hardly anybody said anything after it was announced. Widespread acceptance of this is more dangerous today, because it follows widespread acceptance of two other things—executive orders, and federal agency rules and regulations.

Successive administrations in the White House have issued more and more executive orders as law, and federal agencies have issued more and more rules and regulations as law. Both of these exploded under the Obama administration, where Congress also gave up its constitutional authority to create treaties, allowing Obama to make treaties and reach agreements with other nations on his own.

Americans have accepted the executive branch issues orders as law, and directs federal agencies which issue all manner of rules and regulations as law. The only other thing needed was acceptance of SCOTUS opinions as law to complete our transformation from a constitutional republic into a totalitarian state.

We began as a constitutional republic with three equal branches of government with checks and balances between them. Our legislative branch had elected representatives who were responsible for making the laws we all must agree to live under. Our judicial branch was responsible for applying those laws, and our executive branch for enforcing them.

We now have an executive branch under one supreme leader which not only enforces the law but also makes the law by executive order. It enforces as law the rules and regulations of the federal agencies it directs. It enforces as law the opinions of the members it appoints to the judicial branch. When the executive in this government makes, applies, and enforces the law, it has become by definition a dictatorship or totalitarian state. It is no longer a republic with any need for a constitution.

Many Americans began looking for a single messianic figure to place all hope for change in with Obama, and too many today have a blind, fanatical attachment to politicians. Americans have been maneuvered into the very position the German people were in before Hitler came into power. The only thing lacking in our descent into a totalitarian state is more visible enforcement of executive branch laws.

Members of the American military fought and bled out their lives to defend and protect this country and the world from totalitarian rule and dictatorship under Nazism, communism, and now Islam. These were mostly external enemies or "foreign" as it reads in the oaths taken by those who served. Meanwhile, the enemies "domestic," also referred to in those oaths, have been transforming our nation into another totalitarian state.

If they have *Obergefell* enforced as law they succeed in that transformation.

As I wrote these pages, a particularly ugly presidential campaign came to an end. Americans were told, again, they had to vote for the two remaining candidates because the winner would be appointing several SCOTUS justices during his or her term in office.

I will be surprised if President Trump does not continue issuing executive orders as law, and enforcing federal agency rules and regulations and Supreme Court opinions as law.

Unless you tell him it is not his function to enforce SCOTUS opinions like *Obergefell* as law, it won't matter who sits in the White House.

Unless you tell the members of the Supreme Court it is not their function to make our laws through opinions like *Obergefell*, it won't matter who sits on the Court either.

(5.4) TRANSFORMATION INTO A SOCIALIST TOTALITARIAN STATE

The story goes that as he left the Constitutional Convention in September of 1787, Benjamin Franklin was asked what kind of government the American people had been given.

"A republic, if you can keep it," he replied.

Americans have been referring to our form of government as a democracy rather than a republic for decades. This has been encouraged through progressive education in our government schools. Few students today could explain the difference between a constitutional republic and a democracy.

Progressives believe they are moving us toward a better form of government with a democracy, away from our constitutional republic. We don't need a constitution; we don't need elected representatives; we just need a few progressives in positions of authority to run things.

A republic, like the one we began with, is a form of government in which people elect representatives to make law. In our constitutional republic we have a separation of powers in three branches of government with checks and balances between them. We live under law and the rule of law. We elect people we hope will have the wisdom to create and enforce law.

A democracy, as Thomas Jefferson said, is "nothing more than mob rule."

Elected representatives are required to have the wisdom to consider whether a law is in the common good, and the effects and consequences of a law for the people who must live under it. The primary requirement for being in a mob is that you have less than average intelligence—the less the better. Mobs are like herds, and herds are what animals that spend more time grazing than thinking travel in.

Mobs are fickle, to use an old term. Mob rule is rule by force. Mobs act on emotion. Mobs are usually angry and they burn things down. Mob rule is okay as long as you are in agreement with the mob. If you are not, then the mob may turn on you and tear you apart.

We enjoy more liberty and freedoms than any other people in the world as a result of our constitutional republic. More people continue to want to immigrate to this country than any other country in the world as a result of our constitutional republic.

Progressives have also worked to move America from capitalism to socialism. I expect I am like most Americans in not thinking much about socialism until President Obama took office, and we've had all kinds of discussions about socialism since then.

In fact, Merriam-Webster's Word of the Year for 2015 was the suffix –ism.[2] This was chosen because seven words ending in –ism were the words most often looked up in the online dictionary, or the words which had the greatest increase in lookups, during the year. The top two –ism's for 2015 were socialism and fascism. So socialism was something many people were trying to define; and by no coincidence fascism, because many socialists are fascists as well.

Capitalism is an economic system with free markets and private ownership of the means of production. Socialism is a system with more government or state control of production and state redistribution of income and wealth.

The Obama administration worked to control energy production in this country by wiping out the coal industry, attacking other means of fossil fuel production, and throwing billions of dollars away on crony wind and solar energy pet projects which produced nothing. If you control energy, you control all means of production.

We had all manner of schemes to redistribute wealth under the Obama administration, from national healthcare and increasing dependence on food stamps, regionalism under which money from suburbs is transferred in to the cities, changing the tax code, and stealing more from the "wealthy who are not paying their fair share."

I have nothing critical to say about Americans who sign up for Obamacare or rely on food stamps. But there is much to be said about a government gone mad and bad that makes these and much more available as if free for the taking as a means of redistributing wealth and creating dependence on that government.

We have been led from a constitutional republic to a democracy, and we have embraced anti-capitalism and socialism under progressive leadership.

Lenin's Communist Party took control to move the Soviet Union from capitalism to socialism. This move didn't happen quickly enough for the leaders, and under the dictator Stalin, the police state sought to crush all dissent from the people being forced to live under this system. The people dissented, for example, when they suffered mass starvation, and the state put down dissent by putting them in gulag camps or putting bullets in the back of their heads.

In a communist system, the community owns the means of production, and common wealth is to be shared with everyone according to their needs. Under communism there are no classes, in theory, after the working class overthrows the capitalists. Here again there is not to be private ownership of the means of production, and wealth is to be redistributed to the community by elitists rather than the state or government.

Capitalism produces contentment, and communism produces corpses. Capitalism brought running water, heat, and electricity into people's homes. Communism brought agents of the state into people's homes to drag them away in the middle of the night.

German socialism led to a dictatorship in a totalitarian state. Russian communism led to a dictatorship in a totalitarian state. There are those who argue Germany wasn't socialist. Nazi was short for the National Socialist German Workers' Party. The Soviet Union and USSR were short for the Union of Soviet Socialist Republics. So one might at least think these people thought of themselves as socialists, but no matter.

Progressive socialists in America don't want to be associated with Nazis because the world knows what happened in Germany. Progressives are not as concerned about being associated with communists, because Americans are ignorant about the greater suffering and death brought about by communism, which led to the deaths of an estimated nearly 100 million people, including 65 million in China, 20 million in the Soviet Union, 2 million in Cambodia, 2 million in North Korea, 1 million in Vietnam; and 150,000 in Latin America.[3]

Many of the progressives who took over the educational system in America after World War II were enamored with communism and communist leaders. Few students in government schools today who may have learned of the concentration camps in WWII can tell you what happened in the gulag camps which came after.

Progressives are transforming America from a constitutional republic into a socialist totalitarian state. Progressives in America are doing what like-minded people did in Germany in the 1930s and 40s.

So let's compare Nazi Germany and Progressive America.

CHAPTER 6

NAZI GERMANY
AND PROGRESSIVE AMERICA

I am not arguing that progressives in America today are like the Nazis in Germany because both are socialists. But progressives in America today, and the Nazis who came into power in Germany, are like-minded people. They are statists who believe in government, not government where people rule themselves but government of a ruling class. The Nazis wanted a Thousand Year Reich to rule the world. American progressives want a government to rule Americans, and then a world government which will replace the American Constitution.

History repeats itself because we do not know history. We learn history to avoid repeating the worst parts of it. Progressives are doing in America what the Nazis did in Germany, including enabling mass murder. Here, history has already nearly repeated itself.

I will limit my comparison to six areas: The End of Constitutional Rule by Law, The Use of Homosexuals to Silence Opposition, The Cult of Personality Created

Through Media Lies and Propaganda, The State Control of Law Enforcement, The Control of Youth, and The Elimination of Undesirables and Mass Murder.

(6.1) THE END OF CONSTITUTIONAL RULE BY LAW

The German people lived under the Weimar Republic from 1919 to 1933. Their republic had a constitution. They had a parliament, the Reichstag, in which the elected representatives of the people made law.

In 1933, after a fire in the Reichstag, the Reichstag Fire Decree was issued. Adolf Hitler had been named Chancellor, or head of the government, shortly before the fire. The decree suspended several articles of the constitution, and as the text of the decree on Wikipedia states, made it:

> [P]ermissible to restrict the rights of personal freedom
> . . . freedom of (opinion) expression, including the
> freedom of the press, the freedom to organize and
> assemble, the privacy of postal, telegraphic and
> telephonic communications. Warrants for House
> searches, orders for confiscations as well as restrictions
> on property, are also permissible beyond the legal limits
> otherwise prescribed.[1]

The decree and its application were open to wide interpretation. Hermann Goering, who was in charge of the main German police force at the time, used it as he saw fit; and the Nazi party began to silence and jail those who opposed them.

In 1933, the Enabling Act was also passed, which amended the constitution to enable Hitler to make laws himself, without the Reichstag.

Likewise in America, we have moved, particularly under the Obama administration, from a constitutional republic to another form of government which has increasingly denied foundational civil rights; and from a legislative branch which doesn't pass laws but allows the executive branch to issue them as orders.

The legislative branch also gave up its constitutional authority to approve treaties, allowing Obama to do what he wished including making his "deal with Iran" and reaching other agreements. Treaty provisions are generally considered law in US domestic courts, so here too our executive branch can now make law.

Congress has given future occupants of the White House the authority the Reichstag gave to Hitler.

As I described earlier, America began as a constitutional republic. It is ending as a progressive totalitarian state. Here too, a smarter, superior group of people have determined the people do not need their Constitution. The people should not decide what laws they want to live under by electing representatives in a legislative body. The President should make law by executive order. The Supreme Court should offer opinions to be enforced as law. A mass of government agencies should create an endless body of regulations and rules having the weight of law for the American people to live under.

When a Democrat is in the White House, the Republicans don't squeal too much about presidential executive orders, because they want to be able to play with them when the next Republican is in the White House; and vice-versa. Obama told Americans repeatedly that he would, and he had to, do things by executive orders because Congress was moving too slowly or wouldn't create law to do some of the things he wanted to do. So our children and grandchildren will live under laws by executive order.

The Supreme Court gave itself judicial review authority to declare laws enacted by our representatives are unconstitutional, and the Court has taken to making law as well. So our children and grandchildren will live under laws created by five out of nine justices.

The Code of Federal Regulations is the published rule and regulation book of federal agencies and departments. In 1960, it had nearly 23,000 pages.[2] At the end of 2015 there were over 178,000 pages.[3] These regulating agencies are supposedly under the direction of the executive branch; and more often than not are used by both political parties to impose their ideology on the American people. So when you have rabid environmentalists, for example, in the White House, the Environmental Protection Agency runs rampant. Increasingly, when our elected representatives do enact laws, they are laws to override the regulations some agency or another put into effect.

In his book, *Three Felonies A Day: How the Feds Target the Innocent*, author Harvey Silverglate estimated in 2009 that you may be committing several felonies each day, because the federal code is so huge and open to interpretation.[4]

You may not know what felonies you are committing tomorrow, but rest assured that if you do get out of line as determined by progressive leadership in the executive branch, the federal government will let you know. They will break you by forcing you to defend yourself, even if you don't spend time in jail.

So our children and grandchildren will live under laws created by federal agencies. Maybe our children and grandchildren will live under laws created by anyone but elected representatives. Maybe they won't need to bother to vote for representative legislators at all.

To have everyone but the legislative branch of our government make law is to end constitutional rule by law, and to end our form of government, just as the Reichstag Fire Decree and the Enabling Act ended the German people's form of government.

In a speech before the Enabling Act was passed, Hitler promised, "The rights of the Churches will not be curtailed and their position vis-à-vis the State will not be altered."[5] Justice Anthony Kennedy, who was in no position to promise anything about what would happen to people of faith after the *Obergefell* decision, should have simply quoted Hitler. It would have been shorter and more clear than what he said (quote in chapter three).

We now have an executive branch created to enforce the law which also makes the laws by executive order. This executive makes appointments to the judicial branch, including its flunkies on the Supreme Court, who tell us what the law is, and also make the laws by mere decision or opinion. So the executive branch becomes a dictatorship.

(6.2) THE USE OF HOMOSEXUALS TO SILENCE OPPOSITION

I am not vilifying homosexuals. I don't want anything I say to lead anyone to think less of people who happen to be homosexual. I have said that homosexual behavior is perverse and abnormal, and I am opposing homosexual marriage, and I will continue to do both.

People who are homosexual shouldn't be looked upon differently than any other sinners. The standing of a homosexual before God is the same as an unrepentant liar, adulterer, or any other sinner.

William L. Shirer's *The Rise and Fall of the Third Reich: A History of Nazi Germany*, first published in 1960, is probably the most respected and widely read work on the subject.[6] Shirer wrote that many of the early Nazis were homosexuals. One of the most important was Captain Ernst Roehm, whom Hitler met in 1919. As an officer in the army which controlled Bavaria, one of the German states, Roehm was able to bring former military into the early Nazi party.

As Shirer writes, without Roehm's help, Hitler "probably could never have got a real start in his campaign to incite the people to overthrow the Republic. Certainly he could not have got away with his methods of terror and intimidation without the tolerance of the Bavarian government and police."[7]

Roehm helped organize the party's first paramilitary group—the Sturmabteilung or SA, also referred to as the Brownshirts. These were the thugs who used brute force in the early years. As Shirer described the SA, "many of its top leaders . . . were notorious homosexual perverts."[8]

Moreover, as Shirer wrote of the early Nazi party itself, "No other party in Germany came near to attracting so many shady characters . . . a conglomeration of pimps, murderers, homosexuals, alcoholics and blackmailers flocked to the party as if to a natural haven. Hitler did not care, as long as they were useful to him."[9]

The homosexual Roehm was Hitler's closest ally in the party's formative years. Hitler later created the Schutzstaffel or SS because he came to distrust the SA, and had Roehm executed in 1934.

One could say Hitler might never have come into power without homosexual thugs like Ernst Roehm working for him in the early years. One thing is certain, no teacher in an American government school would dare suggest anything like that today. No matter though, Hitler obviously had many more heterosexual thugs beating and terrorizing people for him in the early years.

Hitler used homosexual thugs like Ernst Roehm to silence his opposition when he began building his party. Likewise in America today, progressives are using homosexuals to silence conservatives and other Americans with traditional values. They are using homosexuals to silence Christians in America, the group with the most reason to oppose their worldview and their imposition of it on the rest of the country.

William L. Shirer wrote about what happened in Germany. Will a future historian, say an author of *The Rise and Fall of a Constitutional Republic: A History of America*, write something similar some day?

(6.3) THE CULT OF PERSONALITY CREATED THROUGH MEDIA

Hitler relied on the Reich Ministry of Public Enlightenment and Propaganda, and his propagandist Joseph Goebbels, to create and maintain his cult of personality. Goebbels fully developed the use of propaganda and he fed it to the German people through newspapers, radio, motion pictures, and rallies.

Likewise in America, the progressive mainstream media—that is, the major television news networks and the old newspapers—put Barack Obama into office. The fawning adulation of the media for candidate Obama was embarrassing and sickening.

Early media propaganda about Obama praised his skill as an orator. He wasn't just a good speaker, he was a great orator. MSNBC's Chris Matthews told Americans how his leg tingled when he heard the new Cicero speak. This fell apart quickly when people began joking about the candidate's inability to speak without a teleprompter from which he read what others had written for him.

Much of the propaganda was summed up in the campaign slogan, "Hope and Change." Americans were to put all their hope in this single messianic figure who would change America. This was a man who had done nothing of any consequence before campaigning for president, but he was going to change the nation.

The only noteworthy thing the Senator from Illinois had done while in office was to pass on voting or vote against several times, legislation providing for medical care for babies who had survived abortions.

Hitler was a failed painter. Heinrich Himmler was a chicken farmer. Barack Obama was an irrelevant senator from Illinois before setting out on the presidential campaign trail. Hitler would have gone nowhere without the media used by his propaganda ministry; Obama would have traveled no further than two paces down the campaign trail without the progressive media in America.

The media propaganda also compelled many Americans to get behind Obama for president because he was a black man. Electing this man would show the world that America could overcome its racist history and its rampant racism of the day.

The big lie here, which so many Americans bought into, was that the media was working so hard to put Obama into the White House because he was a black man. The progressive media, always fighting to overcome rampant racism and inequality in America, supported the first black man to become president of the United States.

If the media in this country wanted to see a black person become president, they could have paid just a little attention to the presidential campaign of Ambassador Alan Keyes, whom other Americans and I supported in 1996. America could have overcome its racism well before Obama came along, if the media had given Keyes just a bit of the support it would for Obama.

The liars and deceivers in the media who got fully behind the Obama campaign wanted another like-minded progressive socialist, a statist; another Marxist like so many of them, in the White House. If Obama had been the wrong kind of black guy, like Alan Keyes, or Herman Cain in 2012, they would have dropped him in a heartbeat for any white progressive who shared their values.

It was also the progressive media who would continuously attack anyone as racist who disagreed with Obama through the course of his administration. No matter how stupid or destructive his proposals or policies might be, anyone who opposed them was a racist. Obama suggested those who disagreed with him were racist when he didn't get his way several times as well, but this was most often done by the progressive media propagandists.

(6.4) THE STATE CONTROL OF LAW ENFORCEMENT

Hitler named Heinrich Himmler the Chief of German Police in 1936, merging the Gestapo which had been run by Herman Goering since 1933, into the SS. The smaller and local law enforcement agencies had been rolled into the Gestapo by 1936.

The Gestapo became the national police agency. The primary function of the Gestapo was eliminating enemies of the state. It was above the law. As Werner Best, an advisor for the SS on legal and personnel matters at the time said, "As long as the 'police' carries out the will of the leadership, it is acting legally."[10]

Likewise in America, the Obama administration worked to federalize local law enforcement. Anything which could possibly be portrayed as another incident of police racism and brutality was front-page news. We were led to believe that local law enforcement needs to be under more direct control and supervision of the federal government.

Black Lives Matter continued the narrative of racist America and encouraged the murder of police officers, as when members shouted, "Pigs in a blanket, fry 'em like bacon!" at the Minnesota State Fair in fall 2015.[11]

Himmler and Goering ran the Gestapo to enforce Hitler's dictates, not unlike Eric Holder and Loretta Lynch headed the Obama administration's Department of Justice. The Department of Justice was allegedly involved in the IRS targeting of conservative groups, the Fast and Furious gun-running operation, and sued states like Arizona that were trying to enforce existing laws against illegal immigration because the Obama administration wouldn't do it.

The Department chose not to enforce laws the administration didn't approve of, and was particularly keen on enforcing laws that comported to "the will of the leadership," as Werner Best described it. Obama took every opportunity to defend Islam, and it seemed he just could not do enough public relations work for the false religion of Islam while he was in office. So Lynch said in December 2015 that her department was going to take action against people who engaged in anti-Muslim speech. Obama declared climate change is the greatest threat we face today. So Lynch acknowledged in March 2016 that the Department of Justice was considering whether the FBI could prosecute climate change deniers.

(6.5) THE CONTROL OF YOUTH

The Nazis had their Ministry of Public Education and the Hitler Youth movement. The Nazi party, understanding they needed to control and make use of the youth, began organizing groups early in 1922. They needed a ministry and a movement to indoctrinate German youth in party values.

Likewise, progressives in America have dominated the government school system to indoctrinate American youth in progressive values, and offered progressive social movements or causes for young people to join up with.

Nazi party value indoctrination included racism. Today, progressive value indoctrination includes feminism, sex education, multiculturalism and Islam, and political correctness. It does not include critical thinking or lessons in American history or civics. According to the Open Syllabus Project, the fourth most often assigned book for reading at American universities today is the *Communist Manifesto*, while I expect many of those students have likely never read the Constitution from beginning to end.[12]

For decades, students have been taught there is no God, and life is without meaning or only has what meaning you ascribe to it. Disaffected youth in the 1960s found meaning in sex, drugs, and rock and roll. Too many of those who survived went on to teach those of us who followed.

Today young people are offered illegitimate and absurd progressive social causes and movements to commit themselves to. They form little mobs whose members mindlessly agitate and blindly accept everything declared by those who shout the loudest, or other leaders who were some of the worst juvenile delinquents of the 1960s trying to relive their glory days.

Since the community organizer moved into the White House, Obama Youth have joined the Occupy Wall Street movement, with many members who couldn't hold jobs so they had plenty of time to protest about others who had earned their wealth.

They have joined the Black Lives Matter movement because everyone just naturally knows black lives still don't matter in the America that Obama constantly derided as racist, racist, racist; where a black man could never hope to hold a position higher than a junior level janitor in the White House.

It is still true, to an extent, that black lives don't matter in America. But evidence for that claim can't be found in anything the fools in Black Lives Matter stomp their feet about. To see how black lives don't matter you need only consider some of America's progressive social policies.

Black lives obviously don't matter in America where black people were around thirteen percent of the population but had twenty-eight percent of the abortions in 2014.[13] Black lives obviously don't matter in America when inner-city parents aren't allowed any choice in sending their kids to lousy, failing government schools. Black lives obviously don't matter in America when a high percentage of young black men don't have jobs, but jobs and benefits are provided for the illegal aliens that progressives are so hell-bent on continuing to bring into the country.

Obama Youth have joined various sects within the environmental movement. Hitler Youth aspired to fight for Germany; Obama Youth aspire to save the world from climate change. Obama declared climate change is the greatest threat we face. Iran may build and use a nuclear weapon or two, but that is nothing to compare to the threat of climate change. Islam is conquering Europe, but we should focus on fighting climate change while we still have the time because there is so very little time left.

Climate change hysteria is rot. The exposed hoaxes, frauds, and false science claims for climate change have

NAZI GERMANY AND PROGRESSIVE AMERICA

been piling up. Climate change is global socialism. Climate change activists demand more power for the United Nations or some other world government to deal with a catastrophic, impending crisis by taxing or fining nations as a means of redistributing wealth on a global scale.

But the real Hitler Youth in America today are those who have joined the Equality Enforcement Brigades. Here little brownshirts and pinkshirts set out to achieve and enforce equality for all Americans as part of the women's movement, the gay civil rights movement, and the gender identity civil rights movement I described earlier. These are increasingly illegitimate and mindless social causes or movements with militant devotees.

The women's movement lurched into absurdity back when it declared the right to an abortion somehow gave more equality to women. Those today who demand free birth control and abortions be made available to all girls and women as part of national healthcare were championed by Sandra Fluke in 2012 as you may recall. She was the college law student who couldn't afford birth control. These women want to have sex and want other people to pay for their birth control and abortions. I know some men pay women to have sex with them, but paying for people to have sex with other people strikes me as stupid.

The Obama Youth who join the gay civil rights movement and chant about marriage equality are even more ridiculous. They demand we place the same value on heterosexual and homosexual marriages. The sexual activity people engage in as part of a heterosexual marriage is required to produce babies. The sexual activity people engage in as part of a homosexual marriage can never produce babies; and leads to higher incidences of HIV transmission and a host of other diseases. To survive, our nation has every interest in continuing to encourage heterosexual marriage. We have no reason or interest whatsoever in encouraging homosexual marriage.

The gender identity movement Obama Youth have flocked to be part of is not worth spending my time writing about.

The Hitler Youth movement indoctrinated young people in Nazi values. The social causes and movements young Americans can join up with today fill their heads with progressive values and ideology. These causes and movements are just as worthless and meaningless as the progressive values they embody.

The Hitler Youth also encouraged their parents and other family members to adopt Nazi party values. And they sometimes dutifully reported other family members who would not adopt party values to their leaders.

As the author of *Hitler Youth, 1922–1945: An Illustrated History* wrote, "The tracking down of subversives and the maintenance of the Nazis' iron grip on the population unleashed a series of forces which sucked children into the most odious deed. Denunciation of parents by their own children to the authorities became one of Nazism's most shocking by-products."[14,15]

In America we have had this government school movement encouraging students to talk to school counselors about what goes on in their homes, which might be contributing to their depression or other troubles. In recent years we read more news stories about kids being asked about parent's gun ownership, and their religious and political beliefs.

The Nazis strongly encouraged all youth in Germany to join the movement. Likewise in America, progressives want all kids enrolled in government schools where they learn to value progressive values. They rail against private schools, accusing them of taking money out of government education. They can't abide any kind of school choice, because someone might choose to attend a private school or go into homeschooling. They are always concerned about the quality of homeschooling, because it is less likely to include progressive indoctrination.

On May 10, 1933, tens of thousands of books were burned in Germany. The books had "un-German" thoughts and ideas according to the university students with the matches. The students didn't think other Germans should be allowed to read books about ideologies opposed to Nazism.

So too in America we have had years of progressive student protests in universities across the country. Students protest when Christian, Jewish, or conservative commencement speakers or other lecturers are scheduled to visit campuses. They protest until speakers are disinvited

THE CHRISTIAN RESPONSE TO HOMOSEXUAL "MARRIAGE"

or uninvited. If a speaker, often with extra university or personal security, arrives to speak on campus, protesters try to shout them down to stop them from delivering their message and shut down the event.

German university administrators didn't much interfere with the book burnings. American university administrators often look the other way or are too craven to stop the protests; and some administrators and "teachers" encourage and get involved with the efforts to silence what they regard as offensive speech.

American progressive students have taken to silencing people at universities with opposing points of view and ideas. Beyond the universities, people who speak out against homosexual marriage are shouted down as bigots and homophobes. People who speak out against illegal immigration are shouted down as bigots and racists. People who deny climate change should be punished by law. All these people should be punished and silenced. They should not be allowed to voice any opposition to progressive values.

But why must these people be silenced? Shouldn't they be allowed to speak, even if they are wrong in their views and understanding, even if they are lying? Why not let them speak, and then explain how they are wrong? Don't you promote your position more effectively when you are able to explain how the opposing positions are wrong?

These people have to be silenced because, more often than not, what they are trying to say is true, and the people who want to silence them are doing the lying, or have nothing factual to support what they are saying.

Before the shouting down, progressive students and universities developed free speech zones and safe zones on campuses to restrict free speech. On these campuses, when someone says anything which another person finds offensive, usually something "un-progressive" like the Nazi book-burning students' "un-German" points of view; they are committing "microaggressions" against a victim. Microaggressors are to be punished, and the so-called victims increasingly respond with physical aggression in return.

Foolish Americans continue to publicly fund universities where students are sent for indoctrination in progressive values including silencing opposing ideas by shouting them down. Any American university student protesting guest speakers or lecturers, who threatens reprisals if they are allowed to speak, or blocks their access to speak, or who tries to silence them through disruptions and shouting them down, should be immediately expelled without any question or debate.

If they want to take any of their personal items with them on the bus, they should be required to pose for a photo holding a sign that reads "Stupid Nazi Book Burner." Then their photos should be passed out at incoming student orientation sessions the following year, where someone tells new students, "We don't allow students like these here. We discriminate against students who behave like Nazi book burners. While some of you are here at university playing ball, drinking, and having sex; there are grown-ups outside in the real world who are working hard to earn their money. Our government takes some of the money they have earned and uses it to fund this university. These grown-ups would stop the government funding this university if we allowed you to burn books or otherwise silence the free expression of ideas here."

(6.6) THE ELIMINATION OF UNDESIRABLES AND MASS MURDER

In their 2009 documentary, *Maafa21*, Life Dynamics details efforts in America to deal with what was referred to as the "Negro dilemma" after slavery ended. What was to be done with the uneducated, freed slaves? You can watch *Maafa21* on the website at *maafa21.com* for free. The DVD should be in every church library. You'll never find it on a government school library shelf.

In 1862, Frederick Douglass was asked what was to be done with the freed slaves and replied, "do nothing with them; mind your business, and let them mind theirs."[16]

But white elitists were concerned about the impact of freed slaves on the economy, and about insurrection and intermarriage. The Yankees in the North (who fought the Civil War, don't you know, to end slavery?) were also concerned that black people might move northward.

Margaret Sanger advocated for the American eugenics movement, which determined, among other things, the white race was superior and should thrive, while blacks were inferior and should not. Sanger formed the American Birth Control League in 1921 to help eliminate the poor, impoverished, and otherwise unfit; those who should be discouraged from having children.

The film alleges the Nazis got some of their ideas studying the American eugenics movement. Hitler was all about eugenics, murdering members of inferior races including the Jews to make room for his Aryan master race. The film notes the Nazis sterilized 600 children of black fathers and German mothers in 1935. Word about what the Nazis were doing in their little eugenics movement got out, so in 1942 Sanger changed the name of her American Birth Control League to Planned Parenthood.

Planned Parenthood went on to focus its attention on black Americans, building a disproportionate number of its clinics in black and other minority neighborhoods. The film alleges Planned Parenthood targeted blacks and other minorities; Planned Parenthood's response has essentially been that they were building where their services were needed, where the business was, so to speak.

So today around thirteen percent of Americans are black and they have around twenty-eight percent of the abortions, as I noted earlier. Has Planned Parenthood been targeting black babies, or should we just credit the organization's marketing skills?

Do you think the body parts of white babies are worth more than black babies?

Dr. Alveda King is featured in the documentary. She's a niece of Martin Luther King Jr. Alveda King and increasing numbers of black Americans in recent years simply refer to Planned Parenthood and abortion as black genocide.

Elite, white, progressive eugenicists and the founder of Planned Parenthood decided we can place more value on the lives of some people, and less value on others. That's what the Nazi murder spree was all about. That's what abortion is about. Someone decided a human life has more value at one stage than at another; so we can legally end the life of a baby, minutes before it might be born, particularly if that baby is black.

We have accepted that this decision can be made about a stage in human life. The same people who demand ending a human life in the first stages also demand we end a human life in the last stages with assisted suicide or euthanasia. And they keep narrowing the gap between these stages. On one end, babies are aborted because they may have Down syndrome or some disorder, or because they are not the desired sex. On the other end, quality of life judgments move that stage toward the center as well.

There are many people in the pews in American churches, including black people in black American churches, who think poor blacks, or people who are white trash, shouldn't be having babies. More than a few think Mexicans shouldn't be having all those babies either; that's the problem with those Mexicans, you know.

Some of these people were sitting in the pews in Nazi Germany and didn't say anything when undesirables were herded out of the synagogues across the street and loaded into trucks to be taken away.

When people, when a government, is able to put less value on the lives of some people than on others, the most amazing and horrific things can be done. You can turn people who would otherwise appear perfectly normal if you met them on the street into the worst kind of monsters you could imagine.

The extermination camps, particularly Auschwitz, provided a career path for Nazi doctors like Joseph Mengele, one of the most infamous Nazi "doctors." After abortion was legalized, we recognized abortionists in America. These "doctors" perform abortions.

I think Mengele and your typical American abortion doctor are more alike than not. We don't talk often enough about Mengele, and in decades of abortion debate we never talk about abortion doctors unless one is murdered by someone who is said to be pro-life, or an abortion doctor like Kermit Gosnell gets caught.

Despite appearances, there was something very wrong with the mind of Joseph Mengele. One of two things happened to Mother Mengele's son in order for him to do the things he did. His thinking became entirely depraved, demented and unnatural, or he had to entirely dehumanize his victims so the people he did things to were not people, they were not human.

According to the *United States Holocaust Memorial Museum online*, there were three categories of medical experiments carried out on concentration camp victims during World War II. [17] The first were intended to benefit Axis soldiers, and included creating conditions soldiers might face by putting prisoners in low pressure chambers or conducting freezing experiments on them. The second involved using prisoners to test drugs and other treatments for illnesses and diseases soldiers might develop. Here prisoners might be exposed to mustard gas to test antidotes for example.

The third category "sought to advance the racial and ideological tenets of the Nazi worldview." [18] Here, different races were tested to see how they survived contagious diseases, and sterilization methods were tested to determine how best to perform mass sterilization on undesirable races. Here, Mengele searched for twins when the people were herded off the trains at Auschwitz. Experiments were done on twin children, and sometimes when one died the other was murdered immediately after for examination and comparison.

You will note the Nazi doctors performed these experiments on other people, including children, for a good cause. They would bring something good out of this for the soldiers or the master race. They are not so unlike those American abortion doctors who harvest the body parts of aborted babies to put them to good use.

To do what he did to people and to children, Mengele would have had to regard them as subhuman or animals while they were alive; and given no more thought to the person whose body was laid before him on the table than most of us gave to the dead pig or frog we dissected in science class.

I think abortion doctors can be understood in the same way.

I cannot imagine entering a hospital room and encountering a baby which has died from a disease or birth defect, let alone one that was aborted. Encountering a baby which has died is a very disturbing, very profound thing. Yet, we have doctors who earn a living by killing babies before they are born; sometimes by dismembering them, sometimes by partial birth abortions which I will not describe.

To do this, abortion doctors need to remind themselves this is a *fetus*. They don't kill babies, they kill *fetuses*. In the same way, I suspect, some of the Nazi doctors had to remind themselves this was a Jew before them, or someone who was retarded or otherwise unfit.

I cannot imagine entering a hospital room and encountering a baby which has died. What do you do? I mean, a baby has died so you have to take care of it—you have to take care of the baby, right? I don't want to say you have to dispose of, or get rid of, the body or the baby— you have to take care of, you have to take care with, this baby that has died. Don't you? And yet, we have people who are able to cut open the bodies of these babies and harvest some of their parts.

These people would otherwise appear perfectly normal if you met them on the street. In fact, we are to understand the abortionist is just another doctor caring for his patient, who took an oath like all doctors do to cause no harm. Well, I don't think the abortion doctor/patient relationship is always what it is portrayed as by Planned Parenthood and the progressive media either.

Just as the abortion doctor has to think of the baby as something less to do his work, so he has to think of the woman as something less. It must be easier if the woman is black, Hispanic, or white trash. It must be easier if he decides the girl is too young or stupid to be having a child or to raise one on her own. There must be many cases where the abortion doctor judges it would be better for the baby if it was never born, or it would be better for the mother.

Nazi sympathizers don't like talking about Nazi doctors because it leads to the acknowledgment that the Nazis thought of many people as not people, as less than human, which is what Nazi ideology led to. Likewise, pro-choice people don't much like talking about abortion doctors.

The Nazis made the life and death decisions for Germany, and progressives make these decisions for America today. What could go wrong?

The Nazis arrived at a "Final Solution" for the Jewish problem. It looks like progressives in America are achieving their final solution with abortion for the "Negro dilemma" I referenced earlier.

Hitler wanted Lebensraum or living space for the master race. Progressives infesting the American State Department promote abortion in other countries around the world as a means of controlling population growth. They want Lebensraum for snakes, bugs, and some birds. At least Hitler put people first, albeit only the Aryan minority.

The Nazis began with mass deportations of undesirables like the Jews, then mass murder. Hitler and his top leadership wanted to rid the world of the Jews. As Timothy Snyder, author of a 2015 book, *Black Earth: The Holocaust as History and Warning* describes, Hitler could set about murdering Jews only after he had ended other states in Europe. When the governments of other nations were ended by the Nazis, the Jews no longer had the protections of citizenship under law. The property of Jews was often confiscated, leaving them with nothing to pay with for emigration, or to later trade for their very lives.[19]

The Nazis began abusing the Jews in Germany early on, and many emigrated. Many who did not were later deported to other countries, "stateless zones" as the author described them, to be murdered. The Germans took Austria and then Czechoslovakia, ending their sovereignty and their governments, and then they could do what they wanted with the Jews. Many emigrated or were deported to Poland.

Germany and the Soviet Union took over and shared Poland. In their half, the Soviets destroyed the Polish state and sent the Jews to gulags. By 1940, the Jews were being herded into ghettos like the one established in Warsaw. In July of 1942, Himmler decided all the Jews in Poland must die; the Warsaw Jews were deported to Belzec, Sobibor and Treblinka death camps where 1.3 million were murdered.

After Germany went to war with the Soviet Union, there were several states or nations which went through double occupation, first occupied by the Soviets then the Germans. The Nazis found it easy to persuade people in countries like Lithuania and Latvia to turn on the Jews after the Germans had liberated the country from the Soviets. When Jews became non-citizens in a country, the locals took their property and handed them over.

As the author states, "Wherever the state had been destroyed, whether by the Germans, by the Soviets, or both, almost all of the Jews were murdered."[20] Where there was no state there was no citizenship for the Jew. Where there was no state sovereignty, puppet states set up by the Nazis determined who had citizenship, and it wasn't the Jews.

States which retained their sovereignty offered protections for the Jews, and so in later stages could refuse to deport their Jewish citizens when the Nazis wanted them. France retained its sovereignty, where Jews without French citizenship were deported to Auschwitz. So ending nation-states, ending national sovereignty, and undermining or taking away citizenship, enabled the Nazis to murder the Jews and a host of other people.

As the author describes, the SS functioned as the state destroyers. They were sent into Poland and then the Soviet Union to end those states. The SS were not sent in the beginning to murder the Jews specifically, they murdered everyone. More Jews were murdered by various auxiliary police groups than SS.

More Jews were murdered by non-Germans than Germans. The Nazis enabled people of many nationalities to use the Jews as scapegoats, abuse them, and murder them. The SS murdered plenty of Jews as well, but they enabled the murder of many more Jews than they killed themselves. As far as I recall, none of the Nazi party leaders actually killed a Jew (Himmler reportedly had difficulty watching one or two of the shootings he was present at) but they made all the murder possible.

Likewise in America, progressives have worked to undermine American national sovereignty, and to devalue or render American citizenship meaningless. They are also enabling mass murder on a scale far beyond what the Nazis were able to achieve.

As I said earlier, whether or not progressives intended to destroy the institution of marriage does not matter; that has been the effect of their influence and their stupid ideas on public policy. Whether or not progressives intended homosexual marriage as a means of silencing Christians in this country does not matter; that has been the effect of their influence and their stupid ideas on public policy.

I am not saying enabling mass murder is an intention of progressives in America. But that has been the effect of their influence and their stupid ideas on public policy. It is an effect or a consequence of what they do. Progressive intentions do not matter. It is almost a law of nature that if you are progressive you need not consider the consequences of your actions or the effects of your policy. Just do what you do because it feels good. Grown-ups have to consider and deal with effects and consequences.

Long ago we should have stopped excusing progressives by considering they mean well. The welfare state these people brought about caused a great deal of misery, particularly for black Americans; but hey, they meant well. Progressives do things, like everyone else, which sometimes have both bad and good consequences. But it seems inevitable we will always be steered to focus on a single good effect of progressive policy to ignore or not weigh the bad effects at all.

So we have progressive media talking about the good things Planned Parenthood does, which warrant continued public funding, despite the abortions and the harvesting of baby body parts. So what if Planned Parenthood does good things? So what if progressives mean well? It doesn't matter. It doesn't excuse what they do. Hitler thought he was ensuring the survival of the human race. Should we excuse the mass murders the Nazis committed to accomplish this?

CHAPTER 7

PROGRESSIVE AMERICA

I have explained how progressives have done in America what like-minded people did in Nazi Germany.

I have explained how ending nation-states, ending national sovereignty, and undermining or taking away citizenship enabled the Nazis to murder the Jews, and a host of other people.

Likewise in America, progressives have worked to undermine American sovereignty, and to devalue or render American citizenship meaningless. They are also enabling mass murder on a scale far beyond what the Nazis were able to achieve.

(7.1) UNDERMINING AMERICAN SOVEREIGNTY

I have described how progressives have undermined our constitutional republic form of government. They want American government under the Constitution to be replaced by world government under the United Nations or some other form. They have all manner of arguments for world government, including the impending catastrophe of climate change.

I have taken care to this point to refer to progressives in America rather than American progressives. It is more accurate to refer to progressives in America, because that is who these people are. They are progressives first, who happen to be stuck in America. They are citizens of the world, or global citizens; not simply American citizens.

They admire the enlightened, socialist countries of Europe. They cannot condemn America enough as racist, imperialist, and full of ignorant saps who cling bitterly to their Bibles and guns. To ingratiate themselves with our betters in Europe, they constantly remind us of only those darkest periods in American history.

America goes to war against other nations. America is bad. Europe is better. Well, as long as you overlook the fact that the history of Europe is all about nations at war with each other, and Europe gave us both World Wars. Without America there would be no European Union today—Europe would be the Third Reich.

Progressives in America have no more regard for our national sovereignty than they have for our Constitution. They never miss an opportunity to demand we subject America and American citizens to international law, and the opinions of the United Nations or other more enlightened countries.

Progressives discourage the sovereignty of nations around the world. They don't want self-governing nation-states; they want world government. So they want open borders, including in America, where they oppose recognizing and maintaining borders against illegal immigration in every way they can.

Progressives in America are not like the Nazis in Germany in undermining national sovereignty, because the Nazis did not seek to end German national sovereignty. But while we have national sovereignty, we are also a nation comprised of sovereign states.

State Sovereignty

Germany had largely self-governing states, but the Nazis took the authority of the states and transferred it to the central government. Progressives in America have likewise all but ended any recognition of state sovereignty, or what we refer to as "states' rights" in America.

One of the worst mistakes we made in America was sending our money to Washington so the members of Congress could wallow in it like pigs at a trough, and then give some of it back to the states if they agreed to do the federal government's bidding.

Today states are suing to stop the federal government from imposing its will and rule on many matters including implementation of Obamacare, enforcement of immigration laws, and whether girls should have to share bathrooms, locker rooms, and showers with boys in government schools.

The Tenth Amendment of our Constitution reads, "The powers not delegated to the United States by the Constitution, nor prohibited by it to the States, are reserved to the States respectively, or to the people." The Constitution grants limited powers to the federal government. Unless prohibited by the Constitution, all other powers belong to the States or the people.

Progressives have taken authority and power from the states and given it to the federal government to build it up. In progressive America, the states have no authority. Students in government schools are endlessly indoctrinated in civil rights, animal rights, immigrant rights, gay rights, transgender rights, and they have no idea what is meant by states' rights.

The Civil War and Slavery

Progressives have violated and revised the history of the American Civil War to undermine state sovereignty. Convincing generations of American students that we fought the Civil War to end slavery and all Southerners are racists required a lot of lying, denying facts, and revising history.

We did not fight the Civil War to end slavery. Emancipating the slaves was an afterthought.

The Southern states began seceding from the Union because of conflict over tariffs and quite a few other things including slavery, and Lincoln determined the northern states would fight to keep the Union together. The Southern states seceded, and Lincoln went to war to put down the rebellion and keep the United States united. Incidentally, Lincoln didn't want the United States devolving into something like those nations of Europe, so admired by progressives today, who were always fighting with each other.

Prior to the Civil War, government for most Americans was state government. Confederate states called their citizens to war, as the Union states did. Southerners were responding to Northern aggression. Robert E. Lee fought for the state of Virginia; he didn't fight to protect the institution of slavery.

Southerners answered the call of their states and fought to defend their homes. Southerners benefited from slavery, but so did the entire nation's economy. Nobody shouted, "We want to keep our slaves, we want to keep our slaves!" while waving the Confederate flag.

There is nothing in the Constitution requiring states to remain in the Union. The Southern states were within their rights to leave the Union. Elected representatives voted to secede and the states did so lawfully. Under the Constitution, Lincoln should have recognized the Confederate states.

Not so long before our Civil War, the people in the states Lincoln determined must remain in the Union had decided to secede from the British Empire, and fought the Revolutionary War to free themselves.

Lincoln did not have the constitutional authority to go to war against the Confederate states and he didn't seek the approval of Congress to do so. Lincoln denied American citizens habeas corpus, by which they could appeal unlawful imprisonment, and imprisoned members of the press and even Union soldiers who spoke out against the war.

Early in the conflict, Lincoln was willing to allow slavery to continue in the Southern states if it could be prevented from spreading to the new western states. He didn't deliver the Emancipation Proclamation until January 1, 1863—over one year and eight months after the war began. He was compelled as much to deliver the Proclamation because it would cripple the Southern war effort as he was by his opposition to slavery.

Students have been taught since progressive indoctrination began that the non-racist Northern states went to war to end the slavery in the racist Southern states. Nothing is taught, for example, about those people in the northern states who were opposed to slavery, not because it was wrong, but because slavery brought black people into the country.

I am not defending slavery. I simply want you to consider how effectively the issue which led to the Civil War (state sovereignty or states' rights) has been erased from history, and how all Southerners have been branded as racists, whether or not they had any involvement in slavery.

Progressives in America do not want Americans considering the states' rights element of our Civil War, any more than they want Americans considering how most of the constitutional authority for controlling and directing their lives was vested in their state governments and not in a federal government.

Since the Civil War, progressives could not achieve the public policy they wanted through state governments, they had to build up and direct the federal government to get what they wanted done. They needed a federal Department of Education for indoctrination. They needed a federal government to impose abortion and homosexual marriage on states whose citizens were opposed to it.

Lincoln's Congress created the federal income tax in 1861 to fund the war. The federal income tax was later repealed, and then reinstated through the Sixteenth Amendment in 1913. Ever since, federal income tax, and other means by which the federal government takes money from citizens, has been used to build up the federal government as it took nearly all powers from the states for itself.

Progressives in America today do not want and will not allow for reserving power to state government as it is referred to in our Constitution, any more than the Nazis allowed this for the states when they took over.

The Lincoln administration has been referred to as an imperial presidency. Lincoln did more than a few things he did not have the authority to do under the Constitution. It was not by coincidence that President Obama referred to Lincoln as his favorite president.

The end always justifies the means for progressives. This is almost a law of nature with them. For Lincoln, the end of preserving the Union, a good end, justified violating the Constitution; likewise the end of ending slavery.

But the end does not justify the means. These ends should have been arrived at by other means.

We didn't fight the Civil War to end slavery; and all Southerners aren't racists today either.

The Confederate Flag

Consider the Confederate flag.

Progressives insist the Civil War was about slavery and had nothing to do with states' rights. That flag is about slavery and has nothing to do with states' rights. The South fought to defend slavery so they were all racists. People with a Confederate flag today are all racists.

The progressive media have raised the Confederate flag as an issue in every election cycle for as long as I can remember. They always find some state capital or other building where Southerners are arguing about flying the Confederate flag. This issue is always raised as evidence of the continuing racism which is rampant in America, where we still have people who want to wave a Confederate flag.

Most people who rallied under the Confederate flag, during and after the Civil War, did so in defiance of the federal government. Some may have been racists; some wanted to keep slaves; but that is not why they rallied under the flag. Southerners answered the call of their states and fought to defend their homes.

There may be a few racists who want to wave the Confederate flag today, but more of those people have a certain rebel spirit and defiance of federal government rule. Many remember—they choose not to forget—their forefathers who fought and died in the Civil War. Many remember—they choose not to forget—how Sherman burned to the ground everything their forefathers owned on his march through the South.

The Civil War, slavery, and the Confederate flag have been used by progressives in America to put down Southerners since the war. This is not because progressives are concerned that Southerners are racist, but because Southerners have always, and continue to this day, to hold more firmly than Yankees to traditional Christian and American values. The "Bible Belt," as we still call it today, is made up of Southern states.

Progressives are more concerned with putting down people who do not share progressive values than they are with putting down racists. If progressives put down racists, they wouldn't be able to parade them about to convince gullible Americans how badly we need progressives in control because America is so racist.

Progressive stereotyping and bigotry toward Southerners rivals white-black racism in America. Americans voted a black president into the White House. But Southerners will always be stupid, racist, Confederate flag-wavers in progressive America.

Abolition

I said earlier that the end of ending slavery should have been arrived at by other means. Slavery should have been ended in America through the abolition movement, not through a terribly bloody civil war which cost the lives of 620,000 Americans and destroyed half of the country's wealth.

It is important to remember that ending slavery through the Civil War did nothing to end racism in America. The abolition movement confronted both slavery and racism. The abolition movement was led by Christians in America. In the context of the Civil War, progressive educators prefer to lecture about Christians who owned slaves, and point to slavery in the Bible. They are not so much interested in teaching about the abolition movement or Christians who were a part of that.

We ended slavery as a result of the Civil War. Racist solutions for the "Negro dilemma" I referred to earlier were proposed, including send black people back to Africa. Continuing racism, in the south and the north, led to the racial segregation of the Jim Crow laws from the 1890s until around 1965.

Jim Crow Laws and Racism

Progressives constantly remind us of the inherent racism of America using the Civil War and slavery. But the Jim Crow laws would serve at least as well to remind us of racism in America. The Civil War was a long time ago, and all the slaves and everyone who fought in the war are dead. The Jim Crow laws are recent history, and you can still talk with people who lived under them today.

It is quite something to consider slavery in America. It is also quite something to consider that until the mid-1960s a black man in America had to tell his mother, his wife, or his daughter who was hungry that they could not eat in the restaurant before them because they were black. A young boy who was black in America had to remind his grandmother or his little sister that they couldn't go into this park or drink from that water fountain if they were thirsty because they were black.

Progressive educators are more interested in teaching about racism and slavery than racism and the Jim Crow laws. This may have something to do with the fact that their favorite political party enacted the Jim Crow laws. As the American Civil Rights Union authors of a paper entitled *The Truth About Jim Crow* put it, "Jim Crow was Dehumanizing; Jim Crow was Deadly; and Jim Crow was Democratic."[1]

Progressives would rather not talk about the rampant racism of the Democrat party evident until 1965. They prefer to talk about the racism of an America which allowed slavery until 1863. Cruelty was inflicted upon black people under slavery. After slavery was ended, cruelty continued to be inflicted upon black people because of racism, particularly by Democrats until 1965.

And it's always the members of this party who remind us of slavery, and condemn Southern slaveholders claiming they should have known better. Those Southern slaveholders didn't have some earlier time they could have looked back upon to reconsider their cruelty toward black people. Slavery was practiced around the world until then, and more white people have been enslaved throughout history as well.

It is those who inflicted cruelty upon black people under the Jim Crow laws who truly should have known better by then, who should have looked back to slavery themselves and reconsidered what they were doing.

All the talk by progressives about America's racist past as evident by slavery would be absurd if it hadn't been so effective in getting black Americans to line up where progressives wanted them. Black people enslaved other black people in Africa for centuries before white Europeans ever set foot on the continent. Then black people continued to kidnap and sell other black people to white Europeans.

When white Europeans came to America, they brought the institution of slavery with them. We didn't come up with the idea of slavery in America; we brought it with us from Europe. Europe. You know, those nations progressives insist we emulate today, because they're smarter and better than us because we used to have slavery in America?

Those Europeans became Americans and wrote a Declaration of Independence and a Constitution which changed the world. Then those Americans went on to fight a civil war, as progressives tell us, to end slavery. Hundreds of thousands of Americans fought and died to free black slaves, as progressives tell us; yet they continue to condemn America as a racist nation because it once allowed slavery.

(7.2) RENDERING AMERICAN CITIZENSHIP MEANINGLESS

The Nazis did not reserve powers for the states in Germany. Progressives in America have reserved no powers for the states. The Constitution does, but they do not. Statehood is meaningless; and nobody thinks much of themselves as a citizen of a particular state in progressive America today. In fact, in progressive America we are not to think of ourselves as citizens at all.

Our American citizenship is the most valuable thing we have in this life. There are parents around the world who would give anything and everything they have to be able to say their children are American citizens.

Our citizenship in heaven, our assurance of salvation through Christ, is the only thing which one might say is more valuable than our American citizenship. That is beyond price, although it was paid for at the price of His life, suffering, and death on a cross.

Our American citizenship comes at great price as well. The founding fathers declared our independence and put all their lives and the lives of their families at risk when they signed the Declaration of Independence. Most of us are descended from people from other lands who sold everything they had and journeyed to this country, enduring the kind of hardships none of us will ever face. Many Americans bled out their lives in foreign lands defending this country and its citizens.

Progressives undermine and render American citizenship meaningless through illegal immigration, by extending constitutional rights to people who are not American citizens, even by opposing proof of citizenship for voting.

Constitutional Rights for Illegal Aliens

It means nothing to be an American citizen when constitutional rights, and other rights and benefits are extended to people who are not American citizens, who are in the country illegally. And the rule of law and breaking the law means nothing either.

It meant something to be an American citizen when people risked everything and endured great hardship to journey to America, achieved that citizenship, assimilated into the culture and were proud to say they were Americans, and worked hard to provide for their families and to contribute and give something back to America.

It means nothing to be an American citizen when the wretches in both political parties grant amnesty and citizenship to illegal aliens to secure a cheaper work force or more voters for their party. And the rule of law and breaking the law means nothing either, when aliens allowed to remain illegally in the country kill American citizens while driving drunk, or rape or murder them.

Constitutional Rights for Terrorists

It means nothing to be an American citizen when constitutional rights are extended to terrorists from other countries. By definition a terrorist has no rights of any kind under the Geneva Convention or any codes of war or military conduct. That's what it means to be a terrorist. You are operating outside of and beyond any rules, and do not get to appeal to rules and rights when it suits you.

Terrorists from other countries have no constitutional rights, or a right to a trial in an American civil court with a lawyer to represent them. The only right a terrorist from another country may be said to have is a right to humane treatment while awaiting a military trial, and swift execution if found guilty of engaging in terrorism. That is the extent of any rights a terrorist from another country has.

Citizen Voting

Progressives are determined to allow illegal aliens to vote in America. The right and ability to vote is an American citizen's first and most fundamental right. We have a right to vote and to choose our elected representatives, those people who will create the laws we can agree to live under. We can vote to choose people who will create laws which will either uphold or undermine all of the other rights we have as American citizens.

We could elevate citizenship, remind everyone how important American citizenship is; but progressives have all manner of idiotic arguments opposing proof of citizenship for voting. Americans need proof of citizenship for a variety of other unimportant things. But it's just too difficult to require proof of citizenship to vote. It's not worth the effort to ensure that only American citizens are able to vote. Your right to vote, and your American citizenship, are just not as important as getting progressives into public offices by any means. Neither political party has any real interest in ballot box integrity either. Both political parties want to be able to accuse the other of fraud when they lose an election.

Americans at Risk

And what was the response of the progressive Obama administration to the murders of an American ambassador representing the president of the United States, and three other Americans who died defending him in Benghazi, Libya? Some mumbling about a video offensive to Muslims which may have been seen by some of the attackers.

The only reason to say a single word about the video was to offer an explanation for what motivated the attackers; otherwise, the fact they had watched a video was no more relevant than what they had for breakfast that morning. It was absurd to say anything about a video.

But the administration simply could not resist bringing it up, even in the context of considering the murder of an ambassador and three other Americans, because they were so absolutely determined to defend Islam and Muslims above anything else. They just couldn't help themselves.

Yes, four Americans were murdered. But somebody also made a video offensive to Muslims. You can be a serial killer or a child rapist in progressive America, and you might still be redeemable or up for rehabilitation. But if you say something offensive about Islam, you are beyond redemption.

Nobody who attacked the diplomatic compound and murdered the Americans serving in Benghazi should have been allowed to walk out alive.

In undermining and rendering American citizenship meaningless, progressives are putting Americans who travel or serve our country in foreign lands at risk.

Only an American citizen has constitutional rights and protections. If American citizenship is taken for granted and rendered meaningless, of what importance are any constitutional rights and protections? In undermining and rendering American citizenship meaningless, progressives are putting our children and grandchildren at risk.

(7.3) ENABLING MASS MURDER

The Nazis made Jews and others less than human or non-human, and they made them non-citizens by ending the sovereignty of other nations. The Nazis enabled mass murder.

Progressives have determined some people have less value than other people in America; and there are stages in which an individual human life has no value at all. There is no state sovereignty in progressive America, and progressive globalists undermine American national sovereignty. Progressives in America are also enabling mass murder on a greater scale than their Nazi predecessors.

Leadership in America did not recognize or refused to accept the truth of the Holocaust for as long as they could. Leadership failed or refused to respond for as long as they could once they understood mass murder was happening. In 1944, appeals were made to the War Department to bomb Auschwitz or the railway lines leading to it before the Jews being deported from Hungary were transported there. If the camp had been bombed, the lives of hundreds of thousands of Hungarian Jews may have been saved. We will never know. No attempt was made and they were not.

In the same manner, progressive leadership in America today denies and refuses to accept the truth of Islamic conquest and mass murder. While leadership is finally beginning to acknowledge mass murder or genocide is occurring, it appears they will continue to refuse to adequately respond for as long as they can.

The Obama administration enabled mass murder as it enforced political correctness. The administration enabled mass murder by giving tens if not hundreds of billions of dollars to Iran, which will use it to murder Jews and others, to finish the job the Nazis began.

Defending Islam

Progressives in America do public relations work for the false religion of Islam. They cannot seem to defend Islam enough. We are told repeatedly that Islam is a religion of peace, despite the fact it demands those most devoted to it cut off the heads of infidels. We are told repeatedly that Christianity is a religion to be condemned, despite the fact it demands those most devoted to it love their enemies.

Progressives have deemed it is politically correct to condemn Christianity. They condemn Christianity by commending Islam.

Why defend Islam?

Progressives have contempt for people of all religious faiths. To be progressive is to reject religion. Progressives are too intelligent for religious faith.

Progressives would have us believe they are the champions of the oppressed and minorities. Progressives own the American civil rights movements, despite the involvement of many people who were not progressives, but Christians, in the black civil rights movement for example. Progressives are all about civil rights.

The "religion of peace" demands those most devoted to it put homosexuals to death. Progressives will not advance their homosexual marriage pet project in any Islamic nations.

The "religion of peace" demands those most devoted to it deny civil rights to women, certainly any of the civil rights women have in America. Men have a right to rape women, to marry pre-teen girls, to do in large part whatever they want with the women who are their property.

There is no freedom of speech in Islam. There is no freedom of religion in Islam. If you criticize Islam, or leave the faith, you are dead.

Yet progressives, these champions of civil rights in America, defend Islam.

Why defend Islam?

Progressives accuse Christians of being racist. Christians owned slaves, you know. Progressives accuse Christians of being sexist. Christian men have authority over their wives and abuse them or keep them barefoot and pregnant, you know. Progressives accuse Christians who would have the least involvement in government or the political process of trying to establish a theocracy.

We have overcome these abuses, if some Christians participated in them, like slavery when we ended it in America. But the abuses by followers of Islam, an absolute theocracy, are so much exponentially worse, and continue today, including slavery.

But progressives accuse anyone who would speak of any of this of being Islamophobic, racist, and xenophobic.

Why defend Islam?

Because, as the old saying goes, "the enemy of my enemy is my friend."

Progressives in America are enemies of our Constitution and our form of government. Many Americans took an oath to defend our Constitution against enemies, both "foreign and domestic." Progressives in America lead the enemies domestic.

Islam is fundamentally the enemy of the Christian and Jewish faiths, and Western civilization. Sharia law is fundamentally the enemy of the Constitution of the United States, and everything America stands for.

You've seen those "Coexist" bumper stickers progressives often have on their cars (cars that usually look as if they won't make it wherever they're going), those stickers that include symbols for the Christian, Jewish, and Islamic faiths? There is no coexistence with Islam. There is no coexistence for the Constitution with sharia law; it's one or the other.

The Nazi SS went through villages across Europe. They took men, women, and children out to woods or to trenches where they lined them up and shot them in their heads. Another line of people were brought to look down upon the first line of victims before they were shot in their heads. Then another line and another line and another line, until the trench was filled or everyone lay in it.

Progressives in America defend Islam, while Muslim terrorists go through villages around the globe. Women and children are raped, then murdered or taken away to be used as sex slaves. People are put in cages and burned alive or drowned; the throats of others are cut open or their heads are cut off. Bodies are left in shallow mass graves.

The Nazis, fearing people would come to learn what they had done, dug the bodies out of mass graves to dispose of them in the ovens once they started operating those in the extermination camps. They tried to hide what they had done. Muslim terrorists broadcast what they do on the Internet, inviting others to join in the rape and murder sprees.

I thought, over the years as I read the books and watched the documentaries on the Holocaust and heard the Jewish survivors say we must not allow this to happen again, we must never forget, that this could never happen again. After all, we have the technology now; we have 24-hour cable news networks; and everyone has cell phones and Internet access and all that. We would know what is happening.

But we do know what is happening. And people choose to ignore it. It is not something that makes people's list of concerns. It would seem these things do not directly affect them or their lives, so they are not of much concern.

Well, these mass murderers for Islam are coming into America as well. And they will directly affect the lives of Americans soon enough again, as they did on September 11, 2001, at Fort Hood, at the Boston Marathon, in San Bernardino, and in Orlando.

I'll come to that in a moment.

The murderous hatred of the Jew was part of Islam long before the Nazis arrived to establish their Thousand

Year Reich. The Nazis shot most of their victims. Then they took to poisoning by carbon monoxide gas. Finally, they built the extermination camps to murder people in the greatest numbers as efficiently as possible The Nazis desperately sought weapons of mass destruction to use against the Allies in the last days of the war before they were finally put down.

Islamic mass murderers have taken up where the Nazis left off. Anyone who is not part of the master religion should be put to death, like anyone who was not part of the master race in Nazi Germany. Both the master race and the master religion require the death of everyone else. And the Obama administration insisted we give billions of dollars to Iran, which will build the nuclear weapons of mass destruction such as the Nazis sought.

Our sworn enemy Iran has sworn to wipe our ally Israel off the map. Leadership in Iran would use nuclear weapons to destroy Israel and the United States if they could, because that's where the Jews are. Around forty percent of the world's Jews currently live in each country. Muslims in Iran and other Islamic nations continue to rail against Israeli statehood. The existence of the nation of Israel, where Jews are protected as citizens, makes extermination more difficult for them as it did for their Nazi predecessors.

But again, it seems what happens in Israel may not directly affect the lives of Americans today, so it is not of much concern. So let's consider those

Islamic mass murderers coming to your neighborhood soon.

Muslim Immigration

Those progressives in America who do public relations work for Islam are absolutely determined to bring Muslim immigrants into America.

I do not judge or condemn Muslim immigrants, nor do I judge or condemn any followers of Islam. I judge and condemn the false religion of Islam, particularly because of what the devoted followers of this religion do, and what becomes of many of them.

Many Muslims are immigrating into other countries to have better lives, sometimes to save their very lives, like people of other religions and races. I don't question their motivation.

But progressives in America are particularly determined to bring Muslims into America. What motivates them? They say nothing about bringing in Hindus or Buddhists or people of other religions.

Likewise, they are absolutely determined to continue to allow illegal immigration into America across the southern border. They don't say anything about increasing the number of legal immigrants coming into the country, yet they constantly defend illegal immigrants.

Many Christians in America are ignorant or foolish in going along with this.

Consider the Muslim immigration from Syria, for example. Muslim groups are in a civil war in Syria, and many Muslims have immigrated to Europe where they are causing great difficulties that could lead to civil war in countries like Germany.

And yet, we are supposed to take Syrian Muslim immigrants into America as well. Here, as in Europe, there may be mass murderers among them.

It is said that many of these immigrants are economic refugees rather than war refugees; they are emigrating to find a better life. If so, we have no obligation to take any of them in if mass murderers may be among them. We can take economic refugees from other countries which are not as likely to include mass murderers.

We have immigration policy to bring people into America who will benefit America. That is why we have immigration. Period. Grown-ups know we cannot take an unlimited number of economic refugees into the country. Progressives insist we can, but they won't say so directly.

We have brought, and should continue to bring in, people with skills or education or a work ethic which will benefit America. These are the people we should allow to immigrate into the country before those who are immigrating for any of the social welfare benefits we provide.

We are not selecting people to immigrate because they will benefit America; we are selecting them because they are Muslim. An immigrant who is a devoted follower of

Islam is not required by his religion to be a blessing to America. If you are a devoted follower of Islam, you will work against America by implementing sharia law.

There are many Muslims who benefit America by immigrating here. But it is not because they are Muslims. Muslim economic refugees are the last people we should be bringing into the country at this time.

Many Syrian immigrants traveled further to European socialist welfare state countries where they could receive benefits; they have not immigrated to nearby Islamic nations to escape the ravages of war.

We do have an obligation to take in war refugees. But if we are taking in war refugees because their side is losing today in a civil war, will we take as many in from the other side tomorrow when they are losing? Are we taking people from both sides in, to continue fighting here? Or should we expect them to just "coexist" with enemies who may have killed their family members and forced them to leave their homeland to come here?

If Christians believe we have an obligation to help people in other war-torn nations, particularly those involved in civil wars, it seems to me we should be doing something to help to resolve the war rather than just enabling a small number of people to leave the country.

There are plenty of grown-up reasons not to allow Syrian Muslim immigration. At the very least, we might not allow Syrian males between the ages of fifteen and sixty-five to immigrate, making more room for women and children, or women with children. One would think progressive feminists in America would support this.

But progressives attack anyone who wants to limit Muslim immigration as racist, Islamophobic or whatever, because they want to bring as many Muslims into the country as possible.

As I said earlier, the enemy of my enemy is my friend. Another old saying comes to mind: "Birds of a feather flock together." Hitler became fast friends with the Italian dictator, Benito Mussolini. I expect totalitarian progressives and Islamic fundamentalists are able to find things in common to talk about when they meet.

It is an acceptable risk to progressives if a few Islamic mass murderers immigrate into the United States. This is because Muslim immigrants will include those who want to replace our Constitution with sharia law. This is because Muslim immigrants are less likely to assimilate than people of other religions, and to accept and encourage American values.

If you don't think Muslims are less likely to accept American values than say, Buddhists, just ask a daughter in a family devoted to Islam what will happen to her if she decides to marry a young man who is Buddhist or Christian and maybe even considers joining his faith. You'll need to ask her before her father or brothers engage in an honor killing though.

As I said, I don't question the motivation for Muslim immigration. The progressive motivation to encourage

Muslim immigration into America is malevolent. Illegal immigration should be understood the same way.

(7.4) ILLEGAL IMMIGRATION

Progressives are determined to defend illegal immigration into America as well as Muslim immigration. They insist that when we have record unemployment we need illegal aliens to work the jobs Americans won't. They insist that we cannot build a wall or fence to maintain a southern border, despite laws enacted years ago to provide for that. They establish sanctuary cities where immigration laws are not to be enforced.

They compare American citizens who want to deport illegal aliens, returning them to their home countries, to the Nazis who loaded Jews into boxcars to take them to the extermination camps. Are their home countries really that bad? Maybe progressive indoctrination in government schools should include critical examinations of these other countries then, and a bit less railing against America.

You don't hear progressives demanding more legal immigration from other countries like China for example. Around twenty-eight percent of immigrants in the United States are Mexican, while three percent are Chinese.[2] If "un-progressive" policies, or if people who were not progressive had policies that resulted in that twenty-eight to three percent ratio, the progressive shrieking about racism would be deafening.

Illegal aliens are more likely to commit crimes against American citizens. By definition, they are committing a crime in entering the country, which is often accompanied by other crimes, including identification theft and falsifying documentation. People from countries like China who legally immigrate are by definition less likely to commit crimes against American citizens.

But as with Muslim immigration, progressives have decided for all that the risk of crime by illegal aliens is acceptable. This is because American citizenship can be devalued or rendered meaningless, as I explained earlier, when you grant citizenship and constitutional rights to illegal aliens.

Illegal immigration is also used very effectively to undermine the law and the rule of law in America. We have had decades of debate about rights and benefits we should extend to people who break the law. It shouldn't be illegal to be an illegal alien, because we shouldn't have any borders in progressive America in the first place. We don't need borders, we don't need laws, we don't need the rule of law, we don't need a Constitution, we don't need elected representatives—we need more debate about the rights and benefits we should extend to illegal aliens.

We have American citizens, veterans who put their lives on the line when they fought for this country, dying in this country because we don't care about them or for them as we should. They do not receive the medical and other benefits they are entitled to, which they have more than earned. But we have plenty of members of both loathsome political parties who are busy working in government to provide everything we can for illegal aliens.

Progressives will only continue to have us bring Islamic immigrants and illegal aliens into the country.

(7.5) FAILURE TO LEARN FROM HISTORY

I have explained how progressives have done to America what the Nazis did to Germany back in the 1930s and 40s. In Germany there was an end of constitutional rule by law, homosexuals were used to silence opposition, a cult of personality was created through media lies and propaganda, the state took control of law enforcement and youth, and finally there was the elimination of undesirables and mass murder.

We should have learned from that history. We should not have replayed that history in America.

There was a Holocaust so we would see what man is, what man can become, without God. Without God, without a fear of God, he is able to line up millions of his fellow men, women, and children in front of trenches to be shot. He is able to take them from their homes to bring them to extermination camps and herd them into chambers to be gassed and their bodies disposed of in ovens.

We did not see this; we would not learn this. So after the Holocaust, we allowed the rise and spread of godless communism. Many more people suffered and perished under communism, and continue doing so today.

Then we allowed progressives to transform America into a nation without God.

We did not bother to learn from what happened in Europe in the 1930s and 1940s. We have not bothered to learn from what happened in recent history in Europe, and are replaying that again as well.

Since World War II, Europe ended the influence of Christianity. European nations became socialist welfare states, and Europeans stopped having many babies. As their populations declined, socialist leaders in Europe increased immigration to maintain the workforce and taxes to provide benefits for the aging populations.

These immigrants included people from Islamic nations with a very different religion that compels some of them to spread their faith by the sword. Once they achieved sufficient numbers through immigration, they began implementing sharia law in parts of European countries, establishing zones where law enforcement from their host countries could not go to enforce their laws.

While most had no interest in wielding the sword, there has been a great deal of conflict in Europe because many immigrated not to work, but to take the social welfare benefits provided by their hosts. Young Muslim males, raised in a religion that teaches them to regard women as property, where women are to be covered from head to toe, have encountered European women who just don't dress like that. Young Muslim males have taken to groping and raping the women they want.

THE CHRISTIAN RESPONSE TO HOMOSEXUAL "MARRIAGE"

Americans did not learn from what happened in Nazi Germany some eighty years ago. Americans will not learn from what happened in Europe yesterday. Americans will continue to allow progressives in America to continue to do their work.

(7.6) JEWS AND WOMEN

So I am left wondering: what will happen to the Jews, and to the women, in America? Islamic mass murderers will not be satisfied to exterminate the Jews, as well as Christians or Muslim apostates, in Israel and around the globe. They must eventually have them in America too.

Young Muslim males who immigrate to America will not suddenly decide to behave themselves because the women they want are American women, no matter how special some of those American women may think they are.

At that time, it should be remembered that Jews and women in America are in the position they are in because of progressives in America, and the effect of their influence and their stupid ideas on public policy. Progressives are enabling the murder of Jews and others worldwide. Progressives are bringing Muslim immigrants, including mass murderers, into the country.

Most Americans would say that women and Jews in America have benefited from the influence of progressives and their ideas on public policy. Most consider the civil rights movements in America as progressive movements which led to equality and the recognition of civil rights for black Americans, women, and homosexuals.

Understanding their history, Jewish people have supported the civil rights movements in America. They want government to defend the civil rights of citizens because they haven't forgotten what can happen when government denies all civil rights and sets out to exterminate them.

We needed some of the civil rights we came to recognize as a result of the black civil rights movement in America. But the black civil rights movement was not as much the work of progressives as the women's and homosexual civil rights movements were.

While women and homosexuals have benefited from their progressive civil rights movements, they have also been helped to cut their own throats, figuratively speaking. Progressives are bringing Muslims into America, which may include more than a few inclined to literally cut the throats of homosexuals and Jews, as well as women who won't convert or they have no use for.

Progressives in America used the civil rights movements to build up big government. It is one of the functions of progressive government to grant rights to its citizens. Then it has to protect and defend those rights for its citizens. Government gets bigger and more powerful with each right it grants, delivers upon, and defends.

Progressive socialists are very busy today declaring all Americans have a right to a job, to healthcare, to free tuition, to change their gender. There are no limits to the rights Americans are entitled to, and to the size of the government required to recognize, deliver upon, and defend those rights.

It is debatable whether progressives in America cared more about using the civil rights movements to build up people or to build up government.

Progressives have used homosexuals and homosexual marriage to silence Christians and others who don't value progressive values. I think there are plenty of homosexuals who might stop and reconsider whether it's really worth recognizing homosexual marriage if it is done only through enforcing a Supreme Court opinion as law.

And sure, the women's civil rights movement, the progressive feminist movement, brought equality to women in America. Progressives came up with all manner of things to do to bring equality to women in America. They even tried to make women more like men and men more like women so they would be the same.

In the last decade, many more American women have come to regret not marrying and having children, divorcing, having abortions, most of those things their progressive feminist sisters insisted they should do.

One of the primary goals of progressive feminists in America was neutering American males. They had more success in that than in achieving what they defined as equality for women. And this brings me back to my question about what will happen to the women in America.

A sixteen-year-old German girl asked in a video in January 2016 why the government in Germany, and particularly the German men, were not defending the women and girls from the immigrants groping and raping them.[3]

Feminists have convinced American women they don't need men. Divorce your husband if he doesn't meet your expectations. Women shouldn't devote their time or energies to raising children and having families, so they don't need men for mating. Women should be in combat in the military, so they don't need men for that either.

American men have been told they were sexist pigs for decades. In recent years, progressive feminists would have us believe all young American men are rapists. There is no easy evidence for that claim, at least not like the frequent news stories about young Muslim immigrants raping women in Germany, England, Ireland, Sweden, Norway, Denmark, France, and other countries.

Governments in some of those countries have taken to censuring the speech of citizens protesting their immigration policies, as well as directing women to not travel alone, or to stay in their homes at night. I guess they are in agreement with those young followers of Islam who believe women should never be allowed to leave their homes unless wrapped up like a mummy and accompanied by a Muslim male to supervise them.

In the past few years we saw pictures of the alpha male Vladimir Putin riding horse or fishing with his shirt off. These are propaganda, but nonetheless we saw him with his shirt off. Then we saw pictures of Barack Obama golfing, or frolicking at the beach with his shirt off before he went to have an ice cream cone.

Now, there's nothing wrong with golfing—President Dwight D. Eisenhower was an avid golfer. But of course that was after he led as Supreme Commander of the Allied Forces in Europe. He also went into Ohrdruf, the first liberated concentration camp, where he said, "The things I saw beggar description."[4] He went on to bring members of Congress and journalists into the camps to bear witness. He had more than earned his golf time.

American males have been neutered. There was a Promise Keepers movement for men in churches years ago, but that didn't do so much to restore manhood either. Once it was gone, it was gone.

Then we have the United States military. In the past few years, Russian propagandists have distributed photos of Putin, while their cohorts in Iran distributed photos of American soldiers on their knees or crying in a corner.

Now I am indebted to every American past and present who served in our military. Whether they saw combat or not, I am in debt to them because they gave up years of their lives to serve this country and to keep it safe so I could raise my children in it. They have kept my children, and yours, and the ones in your community, safe.

But progressives who have changed the American male have also changed our military. Our military no longer has so much a primary function and purpose of killing others before they kill us. It also functions as a social experiment, a proving ground for civil rights and promoting equality. Our female, homosexual military is supposed to go transgender as well.

We have gone from having men in the military to including other groups in the military while only men were in combat, to including other groups in combat as well. None of these groups were included because they were required or necessary to improve the effectiveness of the military. There is no reason to think lowering standards to allow a woman into combat, who is less likely than a man to be able to carry another soldier off the field, will improve the effectiveness of the military. There is no reason to think someone will be more effective at killing because he is a homosexual. There is no reason to think someone who thinks he is a man on Monday and a woman on Wednesday will improve unit cohesion.

The primary reason these groups were included was to make examples of them. Progressives point to homosexuals who are serving in the military and ask how we cannot support homosexual marriage when these people are serving in the military. Transgender people are serving in the military, so how can you discriminate against them if a boy wants to shower with your daughter?

There are individual women and homosexuals who may improve the effectiveness of the fighting units they are in. But these are individuals. The fact they are a woman or a homosexual is not relevant. If including an individual improves effectiveness, that does not lead to the conclusion that including the group as a whole improves effectiveness.

Unless these groups are improving the combat ranks, there is no reason to include them; particularly if including these groups has an adverse effect.

The United States military is not a toy for progressive indoctrination as our government schools became long ago.

The Obama administration changed the United States military for the worst. I frankly don't know which is more pathetic, those "leaders" in the military and in Congress who didn't say anything while our military was transformed, or some of those "males" outside the military who offer their opinions that our sisters, daughters, wives (maybe even our mothers) should be drafted into combat because that's only fair, and they have equality, and we shouldn't have to go if we don't want to go if there are women who might want to go instead.

Progressive feminists in America who led this women's civil rights movement have done more to neuter males than they have to somehow grant equality to women.

We are replaying recent European history, and I expect we may see a sixteen-year-old American girl in a similar video before long.

Men in America in the 1950s would not have allowed this progressive Islamic immigration. They didn't have video, but I have no doubt about how they would have responded. I'm not so sure about many of the boys in America today.

I think much of what's going on here doesn't bode well for women in America.

As for the Jews, as I said earlier around forty percent of Jews are living in America today. Will Americans turn the Jews over to their enemies?

Americans are betraying the Jews in Israel by funding Iran's support of terrorism and its nuclear development. We also betray Jews, Christians, and Muslims around the world in this.

Anti-Semitism has been rising in American universities for decades, particularly those progressive universities that cater to those stupid Nazi book-burning protesters I described in chapter six. David Horowitz details the Jew hatred in universities at www.frontpagemag.com. There is an ongoing Boycott, Divestment, and Sanctions (BDS) movement attacking Israel, another one of those Obama Youth social movements I described earlier.

Much of the Jew hatred at universities is encouraged by Palestinians, who live and breathe only to hate and murder Jews.

Progressive university students are keen on bigger government and world government. It seems bigger government becomes anti-Semitic. While the nations that joined to form the European Union may not have blatantly anti-Semitic policies, the EU adopted one when it decided in November 2015 to label products which came from areas of Israel taken during the 1967 war "made in settlements."[5]

If the leadership in the EU just put a Star of David graphic on the products, they wouldn't have to pay for the translation costs for "made in settlements." Maybe the EU should require its member countries to pin a Star of David on the clothing of any Israelis who enter their countries as well, to discourage people from doing business with them.

I think much of what's going on here doesn't bode well for Jews in America either.

(7.7) TOTALITARIAN STATE

As I explained earlier, because Christians haven't seen the bigger picture we have not responded rightly to the *Obergefell* opinion. When we see the bigger picture, it becomes clear every Christian in America must respond to this Supreme Court opinion.

Immediately after the opinion, two assaulting forces broke cover: the gender identity and totalitarian socialist movements. Americans thought the Court opinion was not important, accepted it as law, or remained silent. Progressives, who successfully brought this country to *Obergefell*, no longer had to work behind the scenes in these movements.

So conflict has broken out in communities across the country where Obama Youth and other dimwits want to force boys and girls in government schools to share bathrooms, locker rooms, and showers, as well as the general population in any public facilities. In doing so, they think they are fighting discrimination as part of another glorious civil rights movement.

In the last presidential contest everyone campaigned on what they would DO if only we voted them into the highest office in the land. Today the office of the President of the United States is an imperial one, not so distinct from the monarchy it was created to replace.

We began as a nation when our founders declared we had certain inalienable rights including life, liberty, and the pursuit of happiness. The founders put government in a box when they declared those inalienable rights came from a creator, from God. They delivered a limited government through the Constitution, limiting government so it would not conflict with those inalienable rights.

We end as a nation with another form of government, a socialist totalitarian state.

Progressives created this state. They determined the Constitution was not written to limit the government; it was written to provide our rights. I cannot say it was written to provide rights for Americans or citizens, because progressives have not limited the rights derived from the Constitution only to Americans.

Progressives used the civil rights movements, topped off by the gender identity movement, to build their power base and build up government into the socialist totalitarian state it is becoming today. Progressives are more interested in totalitarian government than they are in the civil rights movements they used to transform our constitutional republic into that form of government. They don't care about the people as much as they do about who gets to rule over the people.

If you think I am mischaracterizing progressives in America, or what motivated them in these civil rights movements, then consider gun control.

Because progressives care so much about people, we have abortion and homosexual marriage in America, we are adding national healthcare to Social Security, Medicaid and Medicare, we have amnesty, sanctuary cities, benefits and rights for illegal aliens, and public relations efforts for Islam and terrorists.

Progressives in America also work tirelessly for more gun control. Why is that?

We are led to believe that progressives in America want gun control to protect us. Why take away guns, or limit people's access to them, if not to protect others from people who would use guns against them? Sometimes children are accidentally killed with a gun in the house. Progressives want us to remove the guns to protect the children.

Increasing gun control has done nothing to reduce violence; it has done nothing to protect people.

As John Lott of the Crime Prevention Research Center said in 2012, aside from just one incident, "[E]very public shooting since at least 1950 in the U.S. in which more than three people have been killed has taken place where citizens are not allowed to carry guns."[6]

The one place gun violence has been increasing is in gun-free zones. Yet progressives want to make the entire country a gun-free zone.

They are generally too deceitful to admit it. They talk on about assault rifle bans, while the number of people killed by assault rifles is negligible compared to people killed with handguns. If they wanted to prevent gun deaths, they would ban handguns.

The suggestion that gun control protects people from gun violence is absurd. Consider the gun control implemented in your favorite local restaurant that posts a No Guns Allowed sign in the entryway. How does not allowing patrons to carry guns inside a restaurant protect them? Unless you assume angry diners might shoot a waiter, or a gunfight might break out over the salad bar, how does this gun control protect anyone?

Four kinds of people might be confronted by a No Guns Allowed sign on a restaurant door before they go in to eat. People who don't have a gun with them will read the sign and walk in. People with a gun will read the sign, return the gun to their car, and then walk in. Two other people with a gun will read the sign and disobey it. One wants to keep her gun in case she needs it, and the other wants to use her gun inside the restaurant.

The gun control sign, declaring the restaurant is a gun-free zone, does nothing in any way to protect anyone in the restaurant. The shooter, who is willing to, or intends to shoot others inside, will not be put off by a little sign telling her she can't bring her gun inside. The shooter sees a sign that reads No Guns Inside. The gun-free restaurant is safe for the shooter, not for anyone eating in it.

I don't carry a gun around with me all the time. But in my opinion, people with kids shouldn't patronize any restaurant or business with management that posts a Safe for Shooter sign on the front door.

Progressives are not protecting law-abiding citizens through gun control. Progressives do not seek to protect law-abiding citizens through gun control; they seek to disarm law-abiding citizens. The only people disarmed through gun control are those who obey the laws.

These people took our Constitution and flipped it over. Instead of using it to limit the government, they used it to build up the government to an extent that would appall the founding fathers. They changed our government from a constitutional republic into a socialist totalitarian state.

The American people can change our form of government. The founders acknowledged that in our Declaration of Independence; and the Constitution provides a right to bear arms for that purpose. The founders were required to bear arms to change our government from a monarchy into a constitutional republic, to secede from the monarchy, or the Union as one of those Confederate flag-wavers might put it. They gave us that right to bear arms under the Constitution if we needed to do the same.

The American people have an inalienable right to life and liberty, and a right to defend that life and liberty. The Constitution provides a right to bear arms for that purpose.

Progressives didn't resort to arms to change our form of government. They used lies and deceit instead.

Disarming citizens will become increasingly important as progressives in our totalitarian government have to put down dissent. I described earlier how Stalin had to put down dissent when the Soviet Union was working to move from a capitalist to a socialist system. Progressives will have to do the same in America to maintain the state they have created.

CHAPTER 8

ABOUT THAT CONSTITUTIONAL RIGHT TO MARRIAGE

The first two sentences of *Obergefell* read,

The Constitution promises liberty to all within its reach, a liberty that includes certain specific rights that allow persons, within a lawful realm, to define and express their identity. The petitioners in these cases seek to find that liberty by marrying someone of the same sex and having their marriages deemed lawful on the same terms and conditions as marriages between persons of the opposite sex.

(8.1) THE PROMISE OF LIBERTY

The Constitution promised liberty by limiting our government. That is the liberty we are provided by the Constitution. That is the only promise of liberty our Constitution makes.

The founders did not provide us with a Constitution from which the federal government could concoct an endless list of rights to bestow upon the people.

The founders did not want us beholden to the federal government for our rights. The first rights the founders professed were inalienable rights which did not come from the government and which the government could not take away from the people.

The federal government has taken to recognizing so many rights that those rights have begun to conflict with other rights, particularly with the inalienable ones.

So, for example, a mother's right to choose to have an abortion is in conflict with the unborn baby's right to life.[1] The right of homosexuals to engage in perverse and abnormal sexual behavior, declared a constitutional right by the Court in *Lawrence v. Texas*—that right homosexuals were encouraged to exercise by sanctioning their marriages in *Obergefell*—that right is in conflict with the First Amendment Rights of freedom of speech and freedom of religion granted by the Constitution, in law, to all Americans.

The more rights the government bestows upon us, the more it infringes upon our liberties and our more important, fundamental freedoms.

(8.2) DEFINING AND EXPRESSING IDENTITY

So the petitioners were seeking "to define and express their identity . . . by marrying someone of the same sex."

What?

We are to recognize homosexual marriage, extend all the rights and benefits of marriage to homosexuals, restructure the family, redefine marriage, parent, mother, and father, and encourage young people to engage in homosexual behavior, so homosexuals can define and express their identity?

Do heterosexuals "define and express their identity" through marriage? Is that what marriage is for, defining and expressing your identity?

Marriage is for creating little people, and caring for them and watching as they learn to define and express their identity. That's what marriage is for.

I don't think I define my heterosexual identity with any more confidence as a result of my marriage. In fact, I was quite certain I was a heterosexual before I married.

Both heterosexuals and homosexuals can define their identities as such without marrying to confirm it. They should not define their identity by marrying someone else. If homosexuals aren't entirely certain they are homosexual before marrying other homosexuals, they probably shouldn't.

The petitioners sought "to find that liberty by marrying someone of the same sex." Did the petitioners not have the liberty "to define and express their identity" before marriage? Would they spend their lives in a desperate search for that liberty, if not enabled to "find" it through marriage?

I found my liberty and freedoms were somewhat constrained as a result of my heterosexual marriage. I wasn't free to do some of the things I was before I was married, but it was worth it. But homosexuals find an additional liberty through marriage, which they cannot find apart from marriage? Does marriage allow homosexuals to express their identity in some way they cannot otherwise express it? Are they not fully homosexual, free to express themselves, until they are married?

The Court declared in *Lawrence v. Texas* that homosexuals had a constitutional right to express their identity. Do we really need to do all those other things I listed to enable homosexuals to express themselves?

Are married homosexuals further enabled to express their identity when they raise the children of heterosexuals? No two people in a homosexual marriage can ever have a child without involving one person of the opposite sex in some way. The idea that homosexuals somehow express their identity by raising children is absurd. While they may actively encourage the unfortunate child to identify himself or herself as the product of two people in a homosexual marriage, that is a lie.

Any grown-up knows marriage was institutionalized and encouraged for procreation. Had it not been so, you and I would likely not be here. Marriage is for heterosexuals to express their identities by having children. The idea that homosexuals somehow express their identity by marriage is absurd.

It would have been more accurate to say the petitioners seek to affirm homosexuality by marrying someone of the same sex. Homosexuals are simply more confident there is nothing wrong with homosexuality, and their sexual behavior, as a result of the Court's sanctioning homosexual marriage.

But if identity and expression are so important, will the Court continue to discriminate against pedophiles by not granting them the same liberty "to define and express their identity" as pedophiles? The American Psychiatric Association has already taken steps to reduce the stigma of pedophilia, as they did Gender Identity Disorder and homosexuality before it.[2] Why should the Court not do the same for pedophiles?

What is so important about homosexual identity, other than its application for normalizing homosexual behavior?

(8.3) DEFINING AND EXPRESSING IDENTITY PART TWO

The first movie, *The Gay Civil Rights Movement*, was bad enough. But the sequel, *The Gender Identity Civil Rights Movement*, will be even worse as I have explained. Fewer grown-ups will pay for the price of admission to see this one. And why should they, since the Court has already entirely given away the plot?

The Court declared in *Obergefell* that people have a constitutional right to "define and express their identity." So when the Court hears the case about the large, hairy man who wants to wear women's clothing and pretend to be an ugly woman whose constitutional rights were violated when he was told to get out of the women's bathroom, locker room, or shower at the gym; the Court will affirm he has that right they recognized in *Obergefell*.

The five-year-old girl who wants to be a boy has some sort of constitutional right to identify and express herself as a boy, as the Court ruled in *Obergefell* for homosexuals who wanted to identify and express themselves through same-sex marriage.

The Court doesn't need to hear a case about gender identity; the decision has already been made, much like the decision about same-sex marriage had already been made by Justices Ginsburg and Kagan when they set about marrying homosexuals before the *Obergefell* hearing.

(8.4) THE MORE YOU READ . . .

Those first two sentences are the kind of blather only a judge could write. A responsible legislator would find it difficult to put into writing a law creating a right for people to "define and express their identity." A legislator might have to consider whether that was even remotely in the common good, and what the consequences of such a law might be.

But the opinion only gets worse as you continue to read through it:

> *Under the Due Process Clause of the Fourteenth Amendment, no State shall "deprive any person of life, liberty, or property, without due process of law." The fundamental liberties protected by this Clause include*

most of the rights enumerated in the Bill of Rights. In addition these liberties extend to certain personal choices . . . including intimate choices that define personal identity and beliefs.

So there are "fundamental liberties," like those in the Bill of Rights, protected by the Fourteenth Amendment. Justice Kennedy went on to say, "The identification and protection of fundamental rights is an enduring part of the judicial duty to interpret the Constitution."

Ah, no, it is not. Identifying and protecting fundamental rights is not the function of the Court. There is nothing in Justice Kennedy's job description about identifying fundamental rights. There is nothing about protecting fundamental rights in the description either. Under the Constitution, the legislative branch might identify fundamental rights in law, and the executive branch might protect them by enforcing the law.

Justice Kennedy goes on to assert that this responsibility (the one he should not have taken upon himself) "requires courts to exercise reasoned judgment in identifying interests of the person so fundamental that the State must accord them its respect." So Justice Kennedy, and the other four who signed on to *Obergefell,* understand they need to "exercise reasoned judgment" when they set about to identify fundamental interests the State must "respect." It is swell that they understand they must "exercise reasoned judgment"; but they are not responsible to make any judgments about fundamental interests the state must "respect," reasoned or not.

I have repeatedly wondered if anyone else out there reads Court opinions like *Obergefell* as I read through it. I think the judgment of anyone who signed on to this opinion is questionable.

The Court took it upon itself to provide an additional check upon the constitutionality of laws the legislative branch puts forward. The Court decided we needed this additional check which was not included in the Constitution.

Why don't we have an additional check upon the judicial branch? Shouldn't someone else confirm whether SCOTUS opinions, or laws as we may as well refer to them now, are constitutional? Shouldn't someone evaluate whether the Court exercises "reasoned judgment" rather than poor judgment, someone other than members of the Court? There certainly seems to be a need for this.

(8.5) THE FOURTEENTH AMENDMENT

Obergefell relies on the Fourteenth Amendment. If there was no Fourteenth Amendment there would be no *Obergefell*. Section 1 of the Fourteenth Amendment reads,

> *All persons born or naturalized in the United States, and subject to the jurisdiction thereof, are citizens of the United States and of the state wherein they reside. No state shall make or enforce any law which shall*

abridge the privileges or immunities of citizens of the United States; nor shall any state deprive any person of life, liberty, or property, without due process of law; nor deny to any person within its jurisdiction the equal protection of the laws.

The Thirteenth, Fourteenth and Fifteenth Amendments are referred to as the "Reconstruction Amendments." Mistreatment of African Americans continued after the Civil War, and these Amendments were passed to protect the basic civil rights of African Americans.

The Thirteenth ended slavery, the Fourteenth required due process of law and equal protection of the laws, and the Fifteenth affirmed a citizen's right to vote could not be denied "on account of race, color, or previous condition of servitude."

The Fourteenth Amendment was written to protect the rights of African Americans. It was rejected by Democrat southern states, and Democrats in the north, because it protected the rights of African Americans.

The Fourteenth Amendment was not written to protect the rights of other groups, including women and eventually homosexuals and people with a gender identity disorder. It is in the middle of three "Reconstruction Amendments." It was understood the Fourteenth Amendment was not written to protect the rights of women. If it was, there would have been no need for a Nineteenth Amendment giving women the right to vote. But the Court has applied the Fourteenth Amendment to protect the rights of women as well, most notably in the *Roe v. Wade* opinion.

(8.6) DUE PROCESS & EQUAL PROTECTION CLAUSES

These are the parts of the Fourteenth Amendment which read, ". . . nor shall any state deprive any person of life, liberty, or property, without due process of law; nor deny to any person within its jurisdiction the equal protection of the laws."

I have indicated why I don't think the Fourteenth Amendment applies at all. It wasn't written to protect the rights of homosexuals. Or heterosexual white males like me.

Neither of these clauses apply here either.

First, no state can "deprive any person of life, liberty, or property, without due process of law." It follows that if there is "due process of law," a state may "deprive any person of life, liberty, or property."

States do this all the time. If a woman commits a crime, like murder for example, she can be deprived of all three if the state follows the "due process of law," which includes existing laws against murder, a trial by a jury of peers, and enforcement of the law if the woman is found guilty of murder.

One can also say, if there is "due process of law," a state may "deny to any person within its jurisdiction the equal protection of the laws." A woman spending the rest of her life in jail for murder will not have the same "equal protection of the laws" as a woman who is not in jail. She does not have the same civil rights and liberties as a woman who is not in jail.

All states followed the "due process of law" when they were confronted with demands for recognition of homosexual marriage; and then legislators deliberated and decided to enact a law, or they decided not to enact a law, to sanction homosexual marriage.

States likewise followed the "due process of law" when legislators deliberated and decided to give "equal protection" to homosexual marriages. They were not protecting homosexuals; they were protecting homosexual marriages by recognizing them by law. Heterosexuals were not protected by legalizing heterosexual marriage, the institution or union was.

States likewise followed the "due process of law" when legislators deliberated and decided *not* to give "equal protection" to homosexual marriages. They had no valid reason for doing so, because these marriages do not benefit the state in any way. The state simply incurs costs for providing benefits for additional "married" couples, and eventually married "throuples" as groups of three married people have been described.

States had no reason to grant "equal protection" to homosexual and heterosexual marriages, because these marriages are not equal. They do not have equal value, because two people in a sanctioned homosexual marriage cannot possibly produce children.

This does not mean we must place less value on heterosexual marriages which don't produce children. Why would we do that? Why should we bother to do that?

States are not required to give "equal protection of the laws" to unequal marriages, any more than they are required to give "equal protection of the laws" to a woman in jail and a woman who is not.

The Court was not following any "due process" or "due process of law" when it declared that state laws which didn't recognize homosexual marriages were unconstitutional, and then told us what the law is. The Court was not following the Constitution when it did either of these things.

Second, the due process clause says that no state shall "deprive" someone of their liberty. States which didn't recognize homosexual marriages were not depriving homosexuals of any liberties. Twelve states recognized homosexual marriages before *Obergefell*. The other states were not depriving homosexuals of, taking away, this liberty, it didn't exist in those states. You cannot take away or deprive someone of something that doesn't exist.

Way back when each state made a decision to recognize and provide benefits for marriages, no one decided in any state they would only recognize marriages between heterosexuals because they wanted to deprive homosexuals of their marriage right. I don't believe that lawmakers in a state which did not recognize homosexual marriage tried to deprive homosexuals of the right to marry in other

THE CHRISTIAN RESPONSE TO HOMOSEXUAL "MARRIAGE"

states which later legalized homosexual marriage either. Homosexuals were being "deprived" of nothing when states did not find sufficient reason to sanction homosexual marriage.

Black Americans protested the denial of basic civil rights in their movement. Homosexual activists mimicked the black civil rights movement and falsely claimed they were being denied civil rights just as black people had been. This was absurd, but unfortunately was effective. Homosexuals convinced others they were victims, and they were somehow being denied their rights, rights which didn't exist.

They could have reasonably argued for the recognition or creation of new rights, but they achieved more through claiming they were being discriminated against and denied or deprived of their rights.

Homosexuals did not have a "right to define and express their identity" until the Court offered its opinion they should have this liberty in *Obergefell*. They don't have that liberty, and can't claim that liberty either, as a result of a mere SCOTUS decision. But if we pretend there is now a federal law which says homosexuals have this liberty, then one might reasonably apply the Fourteenth Amendment *after* a state had attempted to "deprive" homosexuals of that right.

Homosexuals couldn't wait. The Court couldn't wait for legislators to make laws, so they gave us their opinion to be enforced as law. Progressive social changes must always be implemented quickly, without affording the American people any time to consider what is being done.

(8.7) MEANING AND INSIGHT

But let us pretend for the moment that the Fourteenth Amendment applies here, and return to *Obergefell* which also reads:

> *The generations that wrote and ratified the Bill of Rights and the Fourteenth Amendment did not presume to know the extent of freedom in all of its dimensions, and so they entrusted to future generations a charter protecting the right of all persons to enjoy liberty as we learn its meaning.*

I agree that those generations did not know the extent of freedom "in all of its dimensions" (whatever that means) as we have come to know it when, for example, the Court declared people have constitutional rights to abort and to sodomize. I suppose that those must be examples of "dimensions" of freedom, along with freedoms we provide for illegal aliens from other countries who are not American citizens.

I disagree that there has been some sort of process of learning the "meaning" of liberty. The founders understood the meaning of liberty. And again, the charter protected "the right of all persons to enjoy liberty" by, and only through, limiting government. Moreover, the "extent of freedom" detailed in the Bill of Rights was adequate. It was enough. If the Constitution had been followed, the Bill of Rights would not have been needed at all.

But the Supreme Court came along, and its members have a deeper understanding of "freedom in all of its dimensions."

So *Obergefell* continues:

When new insight reveals discord between the Constitution's central protections and a received legal stricture, a claim to liberty must be addressed. Applying these established tenets, the Court has long held the right to marry is protected by the Constitution.

Apparently one of the functions of the Court is providing "new insight."

Wrong.

Apparently we have a constitutional right to marry.

Wrong again.

(8.8) THE MARRIAGE RIGHT

Obergefell goes on to expound that marriage is "one of the vital personal rights." The "right to personal choice regarding marriage is inherent in the concept of individual autonomy . . . the right to marry is fundamental because it supports a two-person union unlike any other in its importance to the committed individuals."

Obergefell details reasons for protecting marriage and the right to marry, that right as defined by the Court.

As the opinion finally reads: "The right to marry is a fundamental right inherent in the liberty of the person, and under the Due Process and Equal Protection Clauses of the Fourteenth Amendment couples of the same-sex may not be deprived of that right and that liberty."

So marriage is a fundamental right. The Court defined it as such. And, according to this Court's interpretation and "new insight(s)" about the Fourteenth Amendment, homosexuals have the right to marry, because the Fourteenth Amendment does not allow us to deny fundamental rights to anyone.

I won't spend my time debating whether the Fourteenth Amendment really requires that anything defined as a fundamental right must be granted or extended to anyone who wants that right because it's a fundamental one. The Court determined some time ago that anything which could be defined as a right must be granted to anyone who wants it because the Constitution promises that kind of "liberty." That's what the Constitution and the federal government it created are for, in the juvenile progressive view.

I won't spend my time, because I don't have to spend our time, because marriage is not a fundamental or constitutional right.

Heterosexuals do not have a constitutional right to marry. But, according to the latest "new insight" of the Court, homosexuals do.

There is nothing about marriage in the Constitution.

If marriage was a fundamental right, as the Court says, the founders would have included marriage in the Bill of Rights, along with our other fundamental rights.

People were married by law in this country long before we had a Constitution. Heterosexual marriage was recognized and regulated by state laws. It was not granted as a right by law under the Constitution. I can't find a law stating heterosexuals can marry.

Heterosexuals were not given a right to marry by law, any more than homosexuals have been under *Obergefell*. It is simply the opinion of five members of the Supreme Court that homosexuals should have a right to marry. In my opinion their opinion on the matter is irrelevant.

But "the Court has long held the right to marry is protected by the Constitution" as *Obergefell* reads. The Court applied the Fourteenth Amendment, correctly as I understand it, to enable interracial marriage and other marriages among minority heterosexual groups.

Until *Obergefell*, the right to marry which the Court declared was protected by the Constitution was for heterosexuals.

The majority of heterosexuals do not have a right to marry created under the Constitution, but minority groups of heterosexuals have a constitutional right to marry per the Fourteenth Amendment.

It was one thing for the Court to say that all marriages between an adult male and female should have equal protections under the law because those marriages are essentially equal in that they include one male and one female. And, in the case of interracial marriages, a black woman is the equal of a white woman, so her marriage should obviously have the same protections.

It was quite another thing for the Court to say that all marriages between two adult males or marriages between two adult females, and marriages between an adult male and female should have equal protections under the law because those marriages are essentially equal, when they are not. As I explained earlier, we have every reason to encourage heterosexual marriage and sexual behavior, and no reason whatsoever to encourage homosexual marriage and sexual behavior.

One might sanction homosexual marriage to normalize homosexual behavior and reduce the stigma for engaging in it, but I fail to understand why we should do this. As a Christian, it's obvious to me we should not.

The Court applied the Fourteenth Amendment to provide equal protection for interracial heterosexual marriages. These are marriages which are equal, and should be equal, because they can benefit society through procreation. The "bigots" on the Supreme Court of the United States continued, however, to "discriminate" against a great many other heterosexual couples, denying them a right to marriage: brothers who want to marry sisters, sisters who want to marry brothers, mothers who want to marry sons, sons who want to marry mothers, uncles who want to marry nieces, nieces who want to marry uncles, adult men who want to marry little girls, adult women who want to marry little boys, to name just a few.

Grown-ups know the members of the Court were not "bigots" in this, and they weren't "discriminating" against those people; they were simply not interfering in states' recognition and regulation of the marriages they chose to sanction.

States chose not to place equal value on all possible heterosexual marriages, and they had plenty of reasons not to. States likewise chose not to place equal value on heterosexual and homosexual marriages. States gain nothing from providing the same benefits to homosexual marriages as they do to heterosexual marriages.

Legislators in some states may have thought they gained something by acceding to the demands and threats of boycotts which homosexual marriage advocates threw at them. In doing so, they only set themselves up for the next round of demands and threats by gender identity advocates.

CHAPTER 9

EGOCENTRISM

No discussion of homosexual civil rights, and even more so gender identity civil rights, would be complete without considering the mental health of some of the people involved in these movements. While homosexuality may no longer be listed as a mental disorder in the DSM, and Gender Identity Disorder may now be described as Gender Dysphoria, many of these people exhibit more than a few of the criteria for diagnosis as having Borderline Personality, Histrionic, and Narcissistic Personality Disorders in my unprofessional and unlicensed opinion.

These people are described in the dictionary as **egocentric**:

1. having or regarding the self or the individual as the center of all things . . .
2. having little or no regard for interests, beliefs, or attitudes other than one's own; self-centered . . . [1]

When you consider the demands which many of these people have placed on the rest of society, it is difficult not to describe them as egocentric to the point of being unable to live in civil society, to the point of madness; or, more bluntly, as selfish, self-centered, and self-absorbed wretches.

We are expected to change our society and culture, our entire way of living, in fundamental ways to meet the demands of these people; and we already have. It was bad enough with the homosexual activists—the gender identity activists want us to change the world for them.

Consider what we have done to meet the demands of homosexual activists, and how we are beginning to meet the demands of gender identity activists.

(9.1) HOMOSEXUAL IDENTITY EGOCENTRISM

Some homosexuals decided there was nothing abnormal or undesirable about same-sex attraction, there was nothing wrong with their sexual behavior, so they set out to affirm this. It was not enough for them to affirm their sexual behavior for themselves, and to seek some measure of tolerance from the rest of society; everyone else in society would have to affirm their sexual behavior as well. Everyone else in society would say the words, "Homosexuality is normal. There is nothing wrong with the sexual behavior of homosexuals."

They were joined by progressives for another American civil rights movement.

- If homosexuals were historically discriminated against, it was because of their sexual behavior. The sexual behavior of homosexuals was discouraged by law and social stigma. The discrimination or some of the forms it took may have been wrong, but it was all about the behavior of homosexuals.

- People were conditioned to forget or dismiss the sexual behavior of homosexuals. Lesbians were used first in the entertainment media to portray homosexuals as no different from heterosexuals in any significant way (and they are not, aside from their sexual behavior) because it wouldn't do to have the public thinking about the sexual behavior of male homosexuals.

- The American Psychiatric Association had to change its classification of homosexuality as a mental disorder. You could hardly have a civil rights movement for people who were diagnosed with a mental disorder. That would be even more ridiculous than a civil rights movement for people who want to engage in socially unacceptable behaviors.

- This was a civil rights movement for another group of people we were led to believe had been discriminated against because they were different, or simply because they were a minority. It had nothing to do with their behavior. Because they were a minority, they had to be defended against the majority which was out to get them because the function of a majority is always to oppress a minority.

- No matter the costs of legislating and enforcing laws, homosexuals would have a civil rights movement to normalize homosexuality. The American people might get tired of the endless demands for rights by victim groups, which trivialize legitimate civil rights movements like the one for black people; but no matter, homosexuals would have their civil rights movement too.

Homosexuality would be normalized, so laws discouraging people from engaging in homosexual behavior had to be removed. Any stigma against engaging in homosexual behavior, particularly from the church, had to be removed. Young people would be taught that homosexual behavior was normal.

- Homosexual activists have influenced sex education in government schools for decades. People who have no children of their own should never have been allowed to influence sex education in schools, particularly when they did so only as a means of furthering their agendas.

- Homosexuals have been determined to teach five-year-olds how to have homosexual sex and "safe sex." Homosexuals have argued for decades they did not "choose to be gay," they were born that way. Many claimed they knew from a very young age (when they were five) that they were homosexual, as evidence they were born that way. It is not normal for a five-year-old to have any kind of sexual attraction to anyone; there is something clearly wrong with a five-year-old who claims they do. There is no reason for anyone to be teaching children about sex in government schools; and to be teaching five-year-olds how to have homosexual sex, which is something none of them could have even imagined for themselves before being taught about it.

- Homosexuals have led many of the anti-bullying campaigns in government schools which became popular in recent years. Fat kids (yes, I wrote that), boys seen as weaklings, and girls seen as tomboys, have been bullied in schools since the first ones were organized. Homosexual activists weren't compelled to go into government schools to prevent the bullying of weaklings like me forty years ago, or fat kids twenty years ago. They never deliver their messages about bullying in schools today without directly telling students or implying there is nothing wrong with homosexuality or homosexual behavior either. They are not in schools to reduce the bullying as much as they are to reduce the stigma against homosexual behavior.

- The writings of homosexual activists, and the online content of homosexual organizations, has been replete with references to "our kids" for over a decade. Discussion of education and schools often includes references to "our kids." These are not the kids of homosexual parents, these are other people's kids who may happen to be homosexual or believe they are. Homosexuals have gone into government schools to normalize homosexual behavior for kids whose heterosexual parents may not have been as inclined to support or encourage their homosexuality. Given that many younger kids may not continue to identify as homosexual as they get older, these heterosexual parents may have no reason to encourage their children's homosexual behavior either, but homosexuals have taken responsibility to do this for them. There is absolutely no reason to allow homosexuals any influence over the sexual education of other people's kids.

Homosexuals wanted to adopt children.

- People naturally want to have children. Homosexuals can't, or at least no two homosexuals can have a child as a result of their union, so they wanted to adopt them.

- Everyone who has raised a child of their own knows children are better raised by a father with a mother. But we are required to overlook that fact and enable homosexual adoption.

- There are no studies I am aware of which clearly indicate children can or cannot be raised as well by homosexual parents. And that's the problem. There should have been studies, and they should have been considered, before we gave "adoption equality" to homosexuals. If two homosexual adults want a child so they can play "family," where one of the parents gets to play an opposite gender role as a father or mother; someone should have seriously considered whether this was a good thing for the child involved before turning the child over to be played with.

We were not allowed the time to consider the matter. There were some debates and discussions, some considerations by state legislatures; but homosexual activists pressed adoption agencies, particularly Catholic ones, to meet their demands and assist them in adopting children until adoption agencies which did not believe they should enable these adoptions were forced to close their doors so no children would be put up for adoption.

- In the last few years, children raised by homosexual parents began speaking out against same-sex marriage. They did not condemn homosexuality, they weren't critical of the people who had raised them; they explained some of the difficulties and the negative consequences for children raised by homosexuals. But the mainstream media had no interest in allowing their voices to be heard.

- Homosexuals adopted children where they could, and then went on to *use* some of those children when they argued for same-sex marriage. It wasn't clear they should have adopted children in the first place, but homosexuals wanted same-sex marriage to strengthen family bonds. The same progressive hypocrites who declared for decades that half of all marriages end in divorce so we shouldn't bother marrying, demanded "marriage equality" for homosexuals because it serves to strengthen family bonds and is better for children. They argued that something as traditional as marriage should be encouraged as the best means of raising children, but couldn't possibly agree that something as traditional as having a father and mother raising children should remain the standard to be encouraged and preferred.

Homosexuals decided all of society would say the words, "Homosexuality is normal. There is nothing wrong with the sexual behavior of homosexuals," or incur their wrath. Those were the choices we were given. Their demands would be met and satisfied, or else.

- So we had hate crime laws with additional penalties when someone committed a crime against a member of a minority group, particularly homosexuals. Hate crime laws weren't part of the black civil rights movement.

- Hate crime laws led to hate speech, with penalties for engaging in speech homosexuals found hateful. This would inevitably lead to restrictions against freedom of speech, but the risk of that was acceptable as long as people who believed there was something wrong with homosexual behavior, or did not accept homosexual marriage, could be silenced.

Finally, we sanctioned homosexual marriage, so the priest or pastor could say the words, "Homosexuality is normal. There is nothing wrong with the sexual behavior of homosexuals. So if anyone gathered here today can show just cause why these _____ (insert *two men, two women, three women,* etc.) should not be joined together, let them speak now or forever after hold their peace."

- We did this by enforcing as law an opinion of five out of nine unelected lawyers on the Supreme Court, including two who should have recused themselves from the *Obergefell* hearing. We affirmed the judicial branch flunkies appointed by the executive branch have the authority to make laws, and submitted ourselves and our children to rule by the executive branch.

- Marriage had been ordained, and then institutionalized over centuries to encourage and direct the sexual behavior of heterosexuals. Marriage is the best means of producing a next generation of emotionally healthy babies to become citizens. It was better to have males marry and have sex with one woman, and take responsibility for raising children; than males having as many sexual unions with as many other males as they could.

- Marriage had already been eroded by decades of progressive feminist work, including a sexual revolution to encourage promiscuity (there's a word no one under 30 years of age can define) and as much sex as possible outside of marriage, and abortion for the consequences. Decades of men ravaged in family and divorce courts have led to the latest men's movement, MGTOW, or Men Going Their Own Way. After observing what happened to their fathers and grandfathers in divorce court, many younger men will have nothing to do with women and wouldn't dream of marrying and having children. This latest men's movement, a backlash against decades of progressive feminism, is suicidal for society and for men. No marriages, no babies, no future; men who don't marry live less healthy and shorter lives.

- Calls for government and the church to get out of "the marriage business" increased during the short debate about homosexual marriage, at a time when both government and the church have every reason to encourage marriage if we want to survive much longer as a nation at all, if we don't want to die off like the nations of Europe.

- Rather than recognizing the importance of marriage as a traditional institution, valued primarily because of the procreative element; we will use it as a means for homosexuals to "define and express their identity." Identifying and expressing oneself is such a fundamental, constitutional right; that we are to redefine marriage to accommodate this right; along with family, parent, father, mother, husband, and wife.

(9.2) GENDER IDENTITY EGOCENTRISM

As I have explained, the Court declared in *Obergefell* that people have a right under our Constitution to "define and express their identity." In my lifetime, we have been granted some kind of right to privacy, to abort, to sodomize, and now this by the members of the Court. Along the way we were granted some sort of right to government health care as well.

Oddly, the people who demanded these rights are the same people who have worked the hardest to deny other rights to Americans, rights included as real words in the Constitution, like "freedom of speech," and a "right of the people to keep and bear arms."

I won't say much about this gender identity movement. It has just begun. It was fully launched after *Obergefell*, when it was understood that Supreme Court opinion would be implemented as "the law of the land." It was inevitable. Without *Obergefell*, there would be no homosexual marriage, and the gender identity civil rights movement could have been laughed off.

Thirty years ago I thought the first homosexual activist I met couldn't be serious. I thought "homophobia" was a joke I didn't understand. Two men want to get married? To each other? Are you serious?

I could probably return to my old college today and find seriously crazy, seriously determined people who will not tolerate anything less than my full and unquestioning affirmation that they are not of the same gender as their biological sex or of the same species as me.

- Just as the homosexual civil rights movement latched on to the black and women's civil rights movements, so the gender identity civil rights movement latched on to the homosexual civil rights movement. This was epitomized by the alphabet game of letters added to the collection of victim groups demanding civil rights: LGB then LGBT then LGBTQ then LGBTQRSTUVWXYZ and on and on it goes.

- There was some debate about elements of the homosexual civil rights movement. There will be no debate about this movement. You might reason with a typical homosexual activist. There is no reasoning with someone who thinks they were born into the wrong species, that they're really a wombat in a woman's body. We encouraged the sexual behavior of homosexuals by giving them a right to marry. We will encourage the mental illness, delusions and insanity, or simply the perverse desires of others by giving them a right to define and express themselves as they see fit. The boy who thinks he's a girl has a right to dress and act like one, and to demand everyone else affirm this. The man who feels better about himself when dressed in women's clothing has a right to access women's bathrooms, locker rooms and showers if he wishes to do so; and if any women object to this, they are the ones "with the problem." We are approaching 100 new pronouns for idiotic gender concepts, and everyone will use and apply the gender pronoun of choice which an individual demands they use, or else.

• Many black Americans didn't much like the way homosexual activists latched on to their civil rights movement. Many homosexuals didn't much like the way transgender people or pedophiles latched on to their civil rights movement. Transvestites and transgender people increasingly dislike the people with the lunatic list of genders who have latched on to their civil rights movement. Each group seems to think the subsequent civil rights movement is illegitimate. And they are.

• Some of the people in this civil rights movement want to deny biological sex altogether. They declare there is something wrong with binary gender people who are either—who are only—male or female. They declare there is something wrong with asserting animals are male or female.

• These people are even more determined than some homosexuals were to get into government schools and teach five-year-olds that their gender may be fluid. A boy who believes he is a boy should be taught to consider whether he is really a girl. Five-year-old boys will not normally ask themselves whether they might be a girl, any more than they will ponder how to have homosexual sex, if these people are not allowed access to them.[2]

- We changed our understanding of marriage, family, and other natural, social constructs to meet the demands of homosexuals. We are expected to change our understanding of male and female, and teach our children and grandchildren to question their very identities as such, to meet the demands of gender identity activists. We are expected to accept greater violations of our rights, more limits on our freedom of religion and freedom of speech as well, as we go along with this gender identity movement.

- What happens in Canada as progressive social change is implemented often foreshadows what follows here. The Canadian government has been moving to criminalize "gender identity or expression discrimination." In 2016, University of Toronto professor Jordan B. Peterson got himself into trouble by refusing to use the new gender pronouns some of his students expected him to. Peterson argues it's one thing for government to tell us we cannot use certain words, quite another to compel us to use them. This is, quite rightly, a free speech issue for him. As a result of refusing to use preferred pronouns, Peterson has been accused of discrimination, hate speech, hate crime, and abusing his students.

CHAPTER 10

THREE DEATHBLOWS

My grandparents told their children about December 7, 1941; the day President Franklin Roosevelt said would "live in infamy."

I will tell my grandchildren about September 11, 2001 and June 26, 2015 and October 1, 2016.

I expect nearly every reader could tell me that America was attacked on the day remembered as 9/11. I expect most readers had not taken much time to consider the SCOTUS opinion announced on that day in June before reading this book. I expect most readers gave no thought to the transfer of Internet control which occurred on that October date as I was writing these pages.

Each of these dates was not just an attack but was a deathblow to the American Constitution. Each of these dates was a signifier that Americans are done with our Constitution, and so with our constitutional republic.

These were deathblows to the essence of America. America did not end as if all the lights had been turned out. We are still here. America still breathes, but only because the signals have not yet reached the heart or the brain.

(10.1) SEPTEMBER 11, 2001

The attack on 9/11 enabled the federal government to put America in a perpetual state of war. Because we are at war, the federal government has been able to do things it would not be able to do if we were not in a state of war.

We were attacked by followers of Islam who hijacked planes and flew them into the World Trade Center and the Pentagon, with another plane crashing in Pennsylvania. Almost 3,000 people died, and the Twin Towers went down.

One day after the attack on Pearl Harbor in 1941, President Franklin Roosevelt signed the declaration of war against Japan.

Seven days after 9/11, President George W. Bush signed the "Authorization for Use of Military Force." Congress authorized the President to use the military against "those nations, organizations, or persons he determines planned, authorized, committed, or aided the terrorist attacks that occurred on September 11, 2001."

Nine days after 9/11, Bush declared a "War on Terror."

There was no nation or group of nations we could declare war upon, like the Axis powers in World War II. This would be a war against an ideology which could be held by individuals or groups living in any nation.

We are now in a perpetual state of war. There is no nation which will surrender, like Germany or Japan, signing some official document to signify the war is over. We cannot define the enemy as another nation, and we cannot define what it will mean to win the "War on Terror."

Most Americans do not know where our fellow citizens are fighting and dying, and they do not know why they are doing so. In the age of nearly unlimited access to information, few know how many Americans are dying or how the war is progressing. We have accepted that we are at war somewhere. We don't even always refer to it as a war. Americans are "fighting against terrorism" or "fighting ISIS" here or there.

This war on terrorism will never end. Our children and grandchildren will always know war and "rumors of war."

As I explained in chapter seven, Republican President Lincoln suspended habeas corpus and imprisoned citizens for exercising their First Amendment freedom of speech. He was able to do these things because America was at war.

Lincoln decided Americans would kill other Americans. Under his administration, the federal government enacted our first income tax. Americans began turning some of what they had earned over to the federal government to fund the war to enable them to kill other Americans. Lincoln enacted the first draft of American citizens, under which those who could pay the federal government another $300 were able to avoid going to war.

We have been taxed to feed the king and his court and fund his wars ever since.

Democrat President Franklin Roosevelt argued he could suspend habeas corpus in World War II because

Lincoln had. He interred tens of thousands of American citizens of Japanese ancestry in camps during the war, as if the Constitution didn't apply to them at all. He was able to do this because America was at war.

The "War on Terror," launched during the Republican Bush Administration, led to the *Uniting and Strengthening America by Providing Appropriate Tools Required to Intercept and Obstruct Terrorism Act of 2001*, also known as the Patriot Act. The Democrat Obama administration later extended parts of the Patriot Act which would have otherwise expired.

The "War on Terror," and subsequent terrorist attacks in America, have led to increased surveillance of citizens, and many have come to believe our phone conversations, Internet use, and other communications are monitored by agencies of the federal government. Yet we trust the federal government is protecting us and doing what is in our country's best interest, and are willing to overlook some undermining of constitutional rights and our liberties and freedoms if we are protected.

Under the Patriot Act, the federal government has done things which potentially conflict with several of our constitutional rights and protections, including using roving wiretaps and expanded surveillance, delaying notification of search warrants until after they have been executed, and using National Security Letters. The Letters have allowed the FBI to demand without a court order that businesses turn over personal data including citizens' phone, email, and other records.

Critics have charged and courts have held that provisions of the Patriot Act have violated Americans' First, Fourth, Fifth, and Sixth Amendment rights. According to a 2007 *Washington Post* article, an internal audit revealed the FBI had "potentially violated the law or agency rules more than 1,000 times while collecting data" since 2002.[1]

It was not the attack of 9/11, but the perpetual war begun as a result, which is a deathblow to our Constitution. We have acquiesced to a state of war which will never end, under which the federal government can chip away at our constitutional rights.

We have forgotten and taken for granted this Constitution and the rights we have living under it. We have not taken notice as those rights have been denied and undermined because we are at war. To make matters worse, we have taught our children and grandchildren nothing about those rights. Most will never read the Constitution. It will be easy to undermine or violate those rights which they are not even aware they have. And we are going to allow the federal government to do this for the rest of our lives, their lives, and those to follow.

Successive leadership in the executive branch has had less and less regard for our Constitution. Americans vote for politicians who will "do things" and promise to provide what they want; rather than act upon the oath they took to protect and defend the Constitution. These people then violate the Constitution by one means or another from the first day they take office.

There is no longer even a pretense of American citizens holding the federal government accountable to the Constitution and limiting it in any way. The executive branch makes, applies and enforces the law today. It appoints its flunkies to the judicial branch. We no longer have a need for the legislative branch.

The executive will always be more inclined to make laws which violate people's freedoms than the legislative branch is, although the legislative branch has done quite a job of that as well. We could always remove those legislators from office, and have laws repealed. When executive will is enforced through the judicial branch, undermining and violating our rights as American citizens, it is much more difficult to undo what has been done because we're stuck with members of the judicial branch for most of our lives.

(10.2) JUNE 26, 2015

Americans submitted to being ruled by men under *Obergefell*; to living under the rule of the executive/judicial branch, not the rule of law or the Constitution.

Americans had done this already under *Roe*, but *Obergefell* was worse. Fewer apathetic Americans could be bothered to consider the opinion. At least it could be said there was a debate after *Roe*, and has been since 1973. Most Americans didn't give any more thought to *Obergefell* by the weekend after it was announced.

With *Roe*, enforcement or application of the "law" was unnoticed; those women who wanted abortions found their way into those places which provided them. Enforcement of *Obergefell* began years before the opinion, and by the time it was delivered it was widely expected to affect pastors and churches.

As I have explained, for Christians *Obergefell* can be understood as part of a larger effort to stop the spread of the gospel and to leave God with no more use for America; a means to finally end any and all Christian influence on our government and the direction of the country.

This was a final, necessary victory for political correctness over biblical correctness.

There Ought to Be a Law

Before *Obergefell*, twelve states recognized homosexual marriage by law. All states recognized and regulated heterosexual marriages by law.

The Court decided homosexual marriage should be legal in all states. They gave us their decision, expecting us to be ruled by that rather than a law.

The federal government determined the states could no longer decide what marriages they would recognize by law. Not enough states had decided they would recognize homosexual marriage, so the Court stepped in to ensure that all states would do so.

It would be nice to have a law here, so we're not so blatantly living under the rule of men. More importantly, there should be a law here because people are being penalized for not obeying our rulers on the Court.

People have been penalized for years already for not getting in line with progressives and their homosexual activist tools. People who had disagreeable opinions, and sometimes even voiced dissent, have been penalized; losing their standing, their jobs, and their businesses.

Those who have voiced disagreement have been subject to brutal attacks. It is never merely suggested they are wrong in their thinking or in what they believe. They are homophobic, they are full of hate, they are racist (this is often thrown in regardless of the race of anyone involved), they are evil; they want to physically harm homosexuals, and send them to gas chambers like the Nazis did with the Jews. Whatever reputation they have in their communities, whatever standing they have, must be destroyed.

Someone decided along the way that anyone who owns a business which provides services for real marriages must provide those services for homosexual marriages, or they should pay fines and, preferably, lose their business altogether.

Some Americans spend all of their adult lives working to create a business, giving up countless hours of their lives, employing other people, enabling them to live their lives and raise their families; however, if these people are found to disagree with homosexuals who want them to affirm there is nothing wrong with engaging in perverse and abnormal sexual behavior, and so doing this should be sanctioned by marriage, these people should have their businesses taken from them, their livelihood and that of their families, and just go away and die somewhere.

Do you remember the appeals for Americans to be more "tolerant" toward homosexuals; more accepting of men having what they describe as sex with other men, and women with women? People who don't believe in homosexual marriage shouldn't be allowed to make a similar appeal for tolerance, they should just go away and die somewhere.

People have been penalized and punished for a decade already for disobeying the Court ruling before it was actually delivered. It's like "future crime" in the *Minority Report* movie.

It would be nice to have a law here, so people are penalized and punished for breaking a law. People shouldn't be punished for disagreeing with the opinion of five unelected lawyers on the Supreme Court. There should be a law here so the penalties will be just. Everyone should know what the penalties are for breaking, violating, or preventing the enforcement of the law. As it happens, some people have lost their businesses for refusing to bake a cake for a homosexual marriage; while others refused to provide photography services and were only fined.

Justice requires equal penalties and punishments here.

Finally, marriage in America has always been recognized and regulated by laws, primarily by state law. In fact, it was recognized and regulated by laws even before there was an America. Why should it not be so now?

Our rulers have decided to redefine marriage to recognize homosexual marriage, to appease homosexuals who want someone to tell them their sexual behavior is acceptable or normal; so we have done this. That should be enough, shouldn't it, assuming we can ever do enough to appease homosexuals? We should not also have to accept that homosexual marriage doesn't have to be regulated under law as heterosexual marriage has always been, should we?

We should have "equal protection under the law" for all marriages as the Court insisted when it declared the Fourteenth Amendment requires all states to recognize homosexual marriages because they recognize heterosexual marriages.

Five members of the Court took it upon themselves to provide "equal protection under the law" for all marriages. This is certainly not something they are tasked to do under the Constitution, but they did so anyway; and they did a poor job of it.

The Court, at least for the time being, continued to allow each state to apply its own laws regulating marriages. Each state can continue to legislate benefits for marriages within each state; and it surely results in unequal protections under the law when some states provide more benefits for marriages than others.

Some states may require employers to provide family leave time, for example, while others may not. Some states may "discriminate" and only mandate family leave time for mothers with children. To further complicate things, two "married" lesbians raising adopted children in one state may both be provided leave time while only one of the pair might in another state.

I can envision all manner of "horrific injustices" which the Court should prevent or protect anyone who wants to be married from, by also offering their opinions with much greater detail on how every state should regulate all marriages in each state. The Court must do much more than it has to provide "equal protection under the law" for all marriages (and to take away any remaining powers reserved for the states themselves under the Constitution).

We should not recognize or regulate homosexual marriage unless we do so under law.

There Can Be No Law

But, as I explained in chapter five, any such law would be unconstitutional.

Maybe that's why the Court decided they needed to sanction homosexual marriage for us, rather than wait for our elected legislators to do it. Maybe not. It's certainly why progressives turned to the Court to "get the job done" though.

You cannot apply or enforce a law sanctioning homosexual marriage without violating both the First and Ninth Amendments of the Constitution. And yes, the state laws recognizing homosexual marriage passed by dimwits in twelve state legislatures are unconstitutional for that same reason.

A law you cannot apply or enforce is no law at all.

There should be a law. But there can't be a law, at least not under our Constitution in this constitutional republic.

Here's a crazy thought: maybe we just shouldn't recognize homosexual marriage.

But I have digressed.

Submitting as a nation to be ruled by men rather than our Constitution and the rule of law, through *Obergefell*, was effectively the second deathblow to our Constitution.

(10.3) OCTOBER 1, 2016

This was not a dramatic deathblow delivered by a sword but something more like a deep cut through an artery, or a blow shattering vertebrae. This attack was more a signifier, a striking at the essence of America, than the other two.

Free Speech Tool

Americans created the Internet.

This was like the invention of the printing press in that earlier age.

The Internet has grown to be the primary and indispensable free-speech tool of our age. Using the Internet, we are able to communicate instantly with people around the globe. Much that is evil is communicated through the Internet, but it is also the most effective means of communicating what is good to great numbers of people today.

We shared the Internet with the world while we controlled it.

American citizens, organizations, and our government, were in positions to put Internet controls into place or effect. We could censor the Internet or control who was able to access or put material on to the Internet. We could limit peoples' freedom of speech on the Internet.

We did not exert much control over the Internet, or use it as yet another means of taxing American citizens. But in other countries like China, as more citizens began using the Internet and communicating about matters their governments didn't want them to, the censoring began.

While it was developed in America, measures taken to control communication on the Internet, or just the Internet as used by American citizens, could be controlled by Americans; by people living in this country under a Constitution that provides a First Amendment right to freedom of speech and a government charged with protecting that right.

On October 1, 2016, Americans gave up some measure of actual and potential US government control or influence over the Internet Corporation for Assigned Names and Numbers. Governance by the US was potentially passed to other governments and organizations like the United Nations.

Proponents favored privatization, taking possible control away from government. It seemed the primary interest was in removing the possibility of control by our government, not necessarily of any and all governments. I expect most of the proponents were adamantly opposed to other privatization efforts, like social security for example, in the US. President Obama worked to pass control, and I think he opposed the privatization of anything when he had an opportunity to do so for eight years. Obama was simply operating on his core belief that everything is better under UN control than US control.

It has been debated how much real control Americans gave up. My point is only that we gave up some measure of control, and that will inevitably lead to giving up more control to organizations or governments with no interest in, or who have an active interest in controlling or limiting, freedom of speech.

These organizations or governments are not limited or directed by the First Amendment of our Constitution, like American organizations and our government could be.

It is suggested countries like Russia, China, and Islamic nations will soon have some greater measure of control over the Internet through the United Nations. These other countries are hardly champions of free speech. The UN is already determined to control what it defines as hate speech around the globe, and to silence climate change deniers and any others who voice opposition to its agendas.

The one nation in the world with the most and the best reasons to defend and promote freedom of speech, created the primary free speech tool of our age; and rather than advancing and protecting that tool and speech, our "leaders" gave it up for potential control by others with no such interests. There was a late effort by wiser members of Congress to prevent the transfer, but they were unable to.

Giving up what measure of control of the Internet we had, was a signifier again that Americans are done with our Constitution and with our constitutional republic. We are not much concerned about that First Amendment right to freedom of speech we were given to protect and to hold for those who will come after us. Most Americans today have little regard at all for those who will come after us.

But Americans can probably be excused for not paying much attention as freedom of speech was disregarded, in the wake of the progressive blitzkrieg against our freedoms of religion and speech in America which has been ongoing for years already.

Many young people believe freedoms of religion and speech should be limited today. Ignorant students have no qualms about silencing anyone they disagree with. There is no need to discuss, debate, argue, or persuade when you disagree with someone—just shut them up. Progressives debate about the best means of silencing those they disagree with—shouting them down; labeling them racist, sexist, homophobic, transphobic; or physically assaulting them if they can get away with it—that is the extent of debate engaged in by progressives today.

Control Tool

I am afraid the effects of the transfer of some measure of control of the Internet will prove to be worse than a loss of freedom of speech.

As I said in chapter four, America is potentially the only obstacle to world government or totalitarian rule and dictatorship. America, our Constitution and our republic, has to go before a world government or dictatorship can come into power.

The second requirement for world government or dictatorship is control of the Internet. Freedom of speech, such as that right given to us by our Constitution, is the second primary obstacle to world government. People's ability to speak out against the tyrannical rule of government has to be limited before you can effectively put that government into place.

The free-speech tool of our age will be transformed into the control tool of our age. You have to control the Internet to control the world. You cannot control the world unless you control some measure of the Internet.

Economies of nations depend upon the Internet for commerce.

People's dependence upon the Internet continues to increase dramatically. We are building the "Internet of Things," filling our homes with toys, tools, and appliances which connect to the Internet. In 2011, Cisco IBSG estimated 50 billion devices will be connected to the Internet by 2020.[2]

There are too many people in America with profound addictions to their entertainment and toys dependent upon the Internet. Take those away, and many of these people will go into withdrawals that make delirium tremens look like a walk in the park.

If the UN, or globalists intent on world government, want more control over the Internet, what is to stop them from getting it? The UN could impose a tax on the Internet, or charge registration fees, to raise money for its glorious campaign against climate change. Why shouldn't the UN tax the world to save the world?

The UN has goals and agendas which directly conflict with the Constitution of the United States. If the UN was able to fund itself by imposing taxes and registration fees on the Internet, so it was no longer dependent upon the contributions of member nations like the US, why would it not simply disregard the influence of this constitutional republic and other Western nations? Why not instead be directed by authoritarian states like China with majorities of the world's population?

When small nations like Slovakia and Hungary seek to protect their heritage, language, and culture; and exercise a small measure of national sovereignty by refusing to accept mass Muslim immigration, the European Union threatens to cut financial support. Nations of Europe will go along with United Nations and European Union immigration policies or else. As Islamic nations continue to exert more influence over the UN and the EU, what's to stop the UN from pressuring small nations by denying Internet access?

Information Access

Efforts to control and censor Internet speech are increasing in the US.

Alternative media, largely Internet-based, overtook old media during the 2016 presidential campaign.

The liars and deceivers in the old, mainstream press and television networks were determined to put Clinton into office as they had been with Obama. There was no pretense of media objectivity in the campaign. This was obvious to even the most obtuse observers, as more Americans turned off their televisions and took to the Internet for information.

WikiLeaks delivered information the public would never have accessed through our old media handlers.

While much of the information disseminated via the Internet may be inaccurate or factually incorrect, it beats the disinformation Americans have been fed by the old media for decades.

The old media did not report some of the embarrassing stories about Trump near the end of the 2016 presidential campaign to warn us about his character shortcomings. They promoted these stories in an effort to suppress the vote. Every voter sickened by the campaign and the candidates, persuaded to stay home on Election Day, helped Clinton.

The Internet has become the primary means of disseminating information beyond the control of the old media influenced by government and corporations.

Progressives, globalists, and Clinton could not afford defeat in the presidential campaign. After the popular vote, they made every effort to influence the Electoral College vote through protests, recounts, and claiming the Russians had influenced the election.

They blamed "fake news" for the election loss. For these people, fake news is any news delivered by alternative media, by any organizations outside the old mainstream media. Any news which is not delivered by the old media, particularly if it includes information progressives don't think Americans should have access to, is fake news.

The Germans have prohibited the publishing of what they define as hate speech for years already. The European Commission requires US social media companies to respond to hate speech posted on the Internet. The European Union requires removal within 24 hours.

These groups are adding "fake news" to the categories of speech they want banned from the Internet. In the US, Facebook has begun flagging fake news and encouraging viewers to report it.

One could excuse the Germans for decades of banning Holocaust deniers, or anti-Jewish or pro-Nazi speech. But in the United States, the hypocrisy is obscene. While I was growing up, educated in government schools, I was told "Thou shalt not censor" by progressive educators many more times than I was told "Thou shalt not kill" by my Sunday school teachers.

Today we have plenty of old media fake news as well, like those stories about epidemic rape on American university campuses, and catastrophic climate change, but the censors will not be flagging those.

The same people who demand access to government schools so they can educate five-year-olds about homosexual sex, and tell boys they can be girls if they want to (they even have a constitutional right to become a girl) will determine what speech and information adults should be protected from.

We have had decades of banning and penalties for hate speech. Censorship is acceptable. It's progressive.

But those who seek to limit the freedom of speech today are not silencing speech which is hateful, speech which encourages hate, or hate-filled speech which might somehow incite violence. These people are silencing *speech they hate.*

AFTERWORD

Readers may have found some of these pages depressing or distressing, may think I am too negative or pessimistic. But this is not so.

Christians should understand my description of the ending of this constitutional republic is just an indicator that, and a reminder of something you already know, the King will return soon.

Most understand as I do, that America is not in Bible prophecy. It is not clearly seen there. That may not mean it is wiped from the face of the earth, but rather that it is no longer significant. If our Constitution is no longer significant, why the upset about the ending of this constitutional republic, the ending of America?

I believe I have adequately explained that this Constitution and this constitutional republic will have to go before we have global governance or a global dictatorship as described in the Bible. I suggest much of what I have written should simply be understood as Bible prophecy coming to pass.

And yet . . .

It was understood by "those in the know," by the crew of the *Titanic*, that the ship would sink. Enough compartments had been flooded with water so the ship would go down; nothing could be done to save her.

Witnesses reported the stern of the ship rose up out of the water before she broke and went into the darkness.

Likewise "those in the know" today understand that America is going down. Too much has been done which cannot be undone. A handful of older crew members failed to pay attention and failed to act when they should have.

This ship will either rise out of the water before it goes down, or it will not.

Disregard all those frauds and fools today with their prophecies and predictions, their messages and dreams from God with secret details about the future of America. Just understand this: the ship may rise up before it goes down, but go down it will.

So President Donald J. Trump is in the captain's seat now.

During the presidential campaign, he promised to "Make America Great Again." But President Trump has no idea how to make America great again. He talked about rebuilding the economy, restoring the military, "draining the swamp," and other good things. But if he somehow delivered on all of his promises, that wouldn't serve to make America great again.

Like most of his predecessors in my lifetime, we put this man in office and have no reason to think he has studied, or even read, the Constitution. We don't really know if he knows anything at all about what he took an oath to protect and defend before taking the office.

It's not his fault. Few if any Americans asked the 2016 presidential candidates any questions about the Constitution. The mainstream media asked very few, of course, because they are all quite done with the Constitution.

Given the oath of office, you would think half the questions during the presidential debates might have focused on the Constitution. Someone might have asked some general questions any 6th grader in an American civics class in the late 1950s might have been expected to answer.

America is the Constitution and the Constitution is America. The only way to make America great again is to revitalize the Constitution. If efforts to make America great again do not include this, she will only sink into the darkness.

Everything I have seen tells me that Americans are done with their Constitution.

Are you?

Respond if you are not: www.SCOTUSProject.com

SCOTUSProject

APPENDIX

THE WISCONSIN PETITION

Governor Scott Walker
Office of Governor Scott Walker

Attorney General
Brad D. Schimel
Wisconsin Department of Justice

Dear Sirs:

We are writing to request our elected representatives of the state of Wisconsin enforce the marriage laws of the state of Wisconsin despite the United States Supreme Court's decision in *Obergefell v. Hodges*.

We are told that, as a result of the Court's decision, same-sex marriage is now the law of the land. The Supreme Court did not deliver a law. The Supreme Court does not have the authority under the Constitution of the United States to make law.

The Supreme Court delivered its opinion on state marriage laws. We are not required to live our lives, or to instruct our children how to live their lives, subject to the opinions of the Court. We are not ruled by the Supreme Court.

Two justices of the Court were performing homosexual marriages before the hearing. None of the justices had the integrity to recuse themselves or demand the other justices do so.

Marriages performed in a state in which the people have decided their laws should recognize those marriages, are quite different from marriages performed in a state which recognizes those marriages only because five out of nine justices polled thought they should be allowed. If the cause of same-sex marriage proponents is just, if their cause is right, they must convince us it is so and our representatives should legislate accordingly.

An opinion of members of the judicial branch does not have the weight of law any more than an executive order by the leader of the executive branch. We are a nation of laws, enacted by our elected representatives; not a nation subject to the opinions of a handful of unelected lawyers. The Constitution and our government are entirely undermined when these opinions are enforced as law.

We will not comply with any agencies of the federal government who seek to enforce upon us the opinion of the Court when this opinion is in conflict with the marriage laws of our state. The laws of our state, enacted by our elected representatives, overrule the opinions of the members of the Court.

So we also call upon the elected officials of this state to protect our persons and defend our rights if we are confronted with federal government enforcement.

All who call themselves Christians in America have a Biblical mandate to submit to the authority of those who rule over us, and to the law; and to support the government which God has placed us under. All who call themselves Americans have in effect agreed to live under this government according to this Constitution, which many have taken oaths to defend.

Enforcement of this opinion as law is an offense against our Constitution and our form of government.

ABOUT THAT RIGHT TO CHOOSE

The "abortion debate" is a fraud, and the "right to choose" is a bigger fraud.

There is no abortion debate. Abortion is not debatable.

Abortion debates occurred in state legislatures before 1973. Abortion was debated, and elected representatives enacted laws accordingly. Abortion was legal in some states and not legal in others.

Then the Supreme Court declared abortion was legal in every state.

Whether the Court had the constitutional authority to do so could have been a subject of debate. The Court did not have the authority to do so.

But the American people allowed a majority of the oligarchs on the Court to tell us what the law is anyway, and we went along with it. That was a foolish thing to do, and the consequences have been tragic.

The American people did the same when the Supreme Court declared homosexual marriage was legal in every state. We went from foolish to frankly stupid in this, and the consequences will go from tragic to worse.

The media have referred to an abortion debate ever since the *Roe v. Wade* opinion in 1973. They have done so, countless times, to convince Americans that abortion is debatable. We are told abortion is something "good people on both sides" can disagree about. Because abortion is debatable (some think it should be legal while others do not) the decision to have an abortion should be left to the woman. She should decide for herself whether it is right or wrong to have an abortion; because abortion is, after all, debatable.

Progressive feminists declare abortion must be legal. Other actions and behaviors can be legislated, made legal or illegal, but not abortion. A woman must have a "right to choose."

This is another of the unlimited number of rights we established this government for the purpose of granting, in the juvenile progressive view. The founders delivered a Constitution to create a government to concoct and grant rights to citizens, even to illegal aliens and foreign terrorists. This inevitably enlarges government with more power and control.

Many Americans have accepted a woman has a "right to choose." A woman does not have a right to choose to murder, to steal, to do quite a number of other things which none of us have a right to choose to do; but she must have a right to choose in the case of abortion.

It is suggested this right to choose, unique to abortion, is some kind of moral requirement. It is somehow wrong not to give a woman a right to choose in the case of abortion, while she is not allowed to make decisions for herself in other actions and behaviors. Granting someone the ability to choose whether to engage in an action or behavior, is somehow morally better than having legislators consider from a broader perspective and determine whether that action or behavior should be allowed by law or not.

Legislators are expected to consider whether making an action or behavior legal or illegal is in the common good; in the best interest of society at large, of everyone. In the case of abortion, allowing a woman to choose to have an abortion has simply led to more abortions; and to greater acceptance of the ending of a human life by one means or another.

This country began with a declaration that we all have an inalienable right to life, a right not granted to us by the government, which therefore cannot be taken away by the government. It ends with the declaration that we do not have a right to life until after we are born, so government must enforce a woman's right to end that life until the last moment before birth. A baby can even be partially born, and have her life ended, to protect a woman's right to end that life.

There is no inalienable right to life if the government can choose to deny that right.

This right to choose is so sacrosanct that nothing can be allowed to come into conflict with it, not even the right to life itself. This progressive, government-granted right is more important than that inalienable, God-given right.

This is why progressives have had to lie, deceive, and manipulate to dehumanize the unborn baby; to frenetically oppose any attempt to assign some kind of personhood to the unborn baby. They are so determined to enforce the politically correct use of the term *fetus* in place of *baby*, when no woman since pregnancy began has ever been heard to say that she feels her fetus moving; because they cannot have any sort of right to life granted to a baby even a moment before it is born because that might come into conflict with the right to end that life, deceptively phrased as the "right to choose."

Allowing a woman to choose whether to have an abortion is morally superior only if you believe, as those who demand it, that granting someone a legal right to do something is always the right or moral thing to do. Granting someone a legal right is an intrinsically moral act. It's the right thing to do. Not granting someone a legal right, when you are able to do so, is the wrong thing to do.

This leads to the position that what is right is my rights and what is wrong is anything which conflicts with my rights, which is the depth of moral thought of most progressives today. What is right and wrong is defined by what I have a right to, and denying me something I think I have a right to is wrong.

But grown-ups know that if someone is allowed by law to own slaves, that doesn't make slavery a moral right. Under sharia law, a male might have a right to own several women as property, beat them when they get out of line, force younger ones to undergo genital mutilation, and use or sell them as sex slaves. So should we trash the Constitution, as progressives are determined to have us do, and implement sharia law? That might be better for savage young males, but would it be better for women, for the common good? We could really have a "war on women" in America if we implemented sharia law here.

If granting a right to choose is morally superior, why aren't more actions subject to individual choice rather than law? Why isn't stealing debatable like having an abortion? Surely it must be. Robin Hood stole from the rich to give to the poor, didn't he? Why am I denied a right to choose whether or not I will steal something, particularly when I really want the item and will likely be able to steal it without getting caught? I shouldn't steal something if I'm likely to get caught; but if I am likely to get away with it, why shouldn't I?

Indeed, at the end of the day, why should we have laws against anything? Why shouldn't we just allow people to choose to engage in this behavior or take that action, rather than imposing a law on them? Do we need laws against stealing or rape or murder? Should we try to prevent stealing or rape or murder, if doing so means we will be forced to limit people's freedoms by imposing laws upon them?

Laws limit people's freedom to choose, because if they understand there will be negative consequences for choosing one action and not for the other, they really can't be said to be free to choose. Legislators make their choice for them, by attaching negative consequences to one action and not to the other.

Why don't we allow more people a right to choose, even if that leads to more stealing, rape or murder? If it's immoral, wrong to deny them a right to choose, shouldn't we grant them that right as often as we can?

If the right to choose is such a fundamental right, don't you think we should extend it to other behaviors and actions? Why just abortion? If it is so right, it seems so wrong to limit the right to choose.

If you will insist there is some inherent merit or value in a right to choose, you should not do so without understanding why progressives demand women have that "right to choose" unique to abortion.

They do not demand because a freedom to choose has merit or value; they do so as a means of encouraging women to have abortions. They do not want abortion to be illegal. They want a woman to have a legal right to choose to have an abortion because they want the woman to have the abortion.

Understand this—if progressives thought women would be more likely to choose not to have an abortion as a result of "choice" they wouldn't demand it. They wouldn't even ask for it. If women were forced by law to have abortions, you would never hear progressive feminists demand a woman's right to choose. Never. Not ever.

The "right to choose" which they demand is limited to abortion.

You will not hear progressives demanding school choice; particularly for black, inner-city parents who desperately want to get their children out of lousy, failing government schools.

You will not hear progressives arguing that citizens have a right to choose whether they will own a gun, or that anyone should be allowed to choose whether they want to provide services for a homosexual marriage. People shouldn't even be allowed to choose to share a bathroom only with others of the same sex.

Progressives constantly seek to limit other people's freedoms, liberties, and choices. They do this by attaching negative consequences to some actions and not to others, much like legislators would.

It may be that we are somehow adding to people's freedom when we grant them a right to choose whether or not to do something rather than legislating it. But not in the case of abortion. Those who demand a woman's right to choose are not doing so because they think choice has merit in itself. They think abortion has merit.

To accept that the "right to choose" has value or merit, you must accept the progressive motivations for demanding it.

You also must accept the absurd portrayal of women having no control over their own bodies if they are denied a right to choose to have an abortion.

A woman is free to choose to have sex, and free to choose to use birth control when she does so.

I am not considering the wisdom or ethics of birth control or various kinds of birth control. Using birth control was declared a right in two Supreme Court opinions. It is another one of those rights granted by government.

Progressives would have us disregard the choices a woman makes, the control she has over her own body, when she chooses to have sex and chooses to use birth control. They portray the woman bereft of choice as having no control over her own body whatsoever. Progressives insist that denying a woman the "right to choose" is forcing a woman to have a baby. Someone forced her to have sex, and forced her to do so without birth control, and then someone comes along to force her to have the baby.

If a woman makes a decision to have sex when she cannot accept the consequent pregnancy that might result, maybe she shouldn't have sex; any more than the man having sex with her if he cannot accept the consequent pregnancy. Maybe neither should make the second foolish decision to have sex with the other without "responsibly using birth control" as progressives describe it.

The progressive "right to choose" is a fraud. The suggestion women are denied control of their own bodies if they are not given a right to have an abortion is a fraud.

If the "right to choose" had some inherent merit we would be applying it more broadly. We might, for example, continue to allow doctors who do not want to perform abortions, and citizens who do not want to provide taxpayer funding for abortions, to choose not to do so. But the same people determined to provide women, especially black women, with a right to an abortion; continue to work to repeal the Hyde Amendment.

The "right to choose" is an even bigger fraud than the "abortion debate" which led to it.

People fluent in Deceit speak about an "abortion debate" and a "right to choose." These terms shouldn't be in the Christian vocabulary any more than gay marriage, marriage equality, homophobia or Islamophobia.

MY RESPONSE TO OBERGEFELL V. HODGES

The following letter was sent to Justice Kennedy on January 31, 2017.

Justice Anthony Kennedy:

I am writing in response to your *Obergefell v. Hodges* opinion delivered on June 26, 2015.

It may be pointless to respond with disagreements after a decision has been rendered and an opinion delivered, but *Obergefell* still demands a response.

Our country, my children and grandchildren, cannot absorb another SCOTUS opinion like *Obergefell.* So I am writing to urge you to retire yourself from the Court.

I suggest you leave, satisfied you have delivered an opinion which will result in significant social and cultural change (as if that was one of your functions as a Justice), and retire to take up fishing or chess.

Or, if you have any, spend more time with grandchildren who will grow up in this country in a generation which comes to believe they have a constitutional right to marry someone of the same sex, and to "define and express their identity" as a female if they are male, as a male if they are female; or as some other laughable and absurd fantasy gender.

In his dissenting opinion, Chief Justice Roberts asked fellow members of the Court, "Just who do we think we are?"

That was indeed the question remaining after *Obergefell*, and I doubt any of your group of five justices of the majority opinion considered it or replied.

So I am writing to ask you directly, "Just who do you think you are, sir?"

I am not ruled by you.

I will not be ruled by you, because I have several children and grandchildren, and they have little friends. I will not leave them behind to be ruled by you without at least saying something about it.

I am not ruled by you because I am an American citizen. As such, I live under the rule of the Constitution and the rule of law. I am not required to live under the rule of you or the other oligarchs on the Supreme Court.

As a Christian, I have a biblical mandate to submit to those in government who have authority over me.

That does not include you.

You do not tell me what the law is. That is the function of my elected representatives in the legislative branch.

In this constitutional republic I am tasked with voting for those responsible to enact the laws I have to live under and raise my children to live under. According to the Constitution only my elected representatives create law.

Your thoughts on homosexual marriage are entirely irrelevant to me, so I will not stand for your decision or opinion being enforced as law in the state in which I reside, which only recognizes heterosexual marriages and provides benefits for those marriages under state law.

Many young people will no longer experience same-sex attraction by the time they reach adulthood.

In its *HIV Surveillance Report, 2014*, the Centers for Disease Control and Prevention reported "the annual number of diagnosed HIV infections attributed to male-to-male sexual contact increased" from 2010 to 2014.

The CDC also notes, "Gay and bisexual men aged 13 to 24 accounted for an estimated 92% of new HIV diagnoses among all men in their age group" in 2014; and projects that "if current diagnosis rates continue...1 in 2 black/African American gay and bisexual men" will face an HIV diagnosis in their lifetime.[1]

But members of the Court decided it was their function to remove any stigma against engaging in homosexual sexual behavior (*Lawrence v. Texas*); and finally and fully normalized the sexual behavior of homosexuals by sanctioning it through marriage with *Obergefell*.

Young men in America are encouraged by the Court to engage in homosexual sexual behavior, which puts young black American men at frighteningly high risk for contracting HIV. The Court earlier legalized abortion for the nation, which has led to black genocide as described by Dr. Alveda King and others. So black babies not eliminated by the abortions encouraged by the Court might still be eliminated when they are older if they are persuaded to engage in the sexual behavior encouraged by the Court.

You continue where others have created additional responsibilities and functions for the Court not even hinted at in the Constitution. This gauntlet the Court has created for black males in America is one of the consequences those of us in the ruled class have to live with. If we can.

In the fifth edition of the American Psychiatric Association's *Diagnostic and Statistical Manual of Mental Disorders*, the APA indicates that only as few as 2.2% of boys and 12% of girls may continue to have gender identity issues into adulthood (DSM-5, p.455).

That information has not yet been stricken from the DSM under pressure from the contemporary Brownshirt activists in the gender identity civil rights movement, as the material homosexual activists found disagreeable was removed from the DSM in the early 1970's.

But members of the Supreme Court decided it was their function—their "duty"—to identify and protect "fundamental rights"; and so declared in *Obergefell* that people have a constitutional right to "define and express their identity" as they see fit.

Adult males who are mentally ill, who are living out some idiotic fantasy, or are simply perverts; have a constitutional right to pretend they are females, and to share any public facilities with females including my daughters.

Apparently you did not consider the behaviors which would be encouraged by *Obergefell*; you were simply jumping on board the progressive bandwagon to advance yet another civil rights movement.

In addition to finally and fully normalizing homosexual sexual behavior, declaring there is nothing at all wrong with engaging in homosexual behavior despite the medical and mental health reasons to at least consider not engaging in that behavior; you effectively launched the gender identity civil rights movement.

Obergefell will do more to wreak havoc on our culture and society than it will ever do to unite homosexuals in marriage.

I assume you knew that Justices Kagan and Ginsburg had already decided same-sex marriage was acceptable and should be legal—they were marrying homosexuals— before the *Obergefell* hearing.

Did you think people like me—in what is now officially the ruled class in this country after *Obergefell*—would not become aware of this?

Did you think it wouldn't matter if we found out— that we might not have the intelligence or awareness to understand how this is an issue?

In the real world, among the ruled class, many of us have to avoid even the appearance of impropriety. We have to avoid any conflict of interest, even the appearance of it, or face disciplinary action by our employers.

Did you think that if we came to understand Kagan and Ginsburg should not have been involved in this decision, we would just overlook that and put our simple faith in the integrity of those two Justices? Do you think we would just accept they would nevertheless make an objective, unbiased, honest decision about homosexual marriage—a decision we should abide by and teach our children to abide by, for the rest of our lives?

Well, this does matter—greatly—because the participation of Justices Kagan and Ginsburg makes the *Obergefell* hearing a farce, a fraud and a sham; and it makes your decision and your opinion a farce, a fraud and a sham.

And it makes every opinion this Court delivers in the future suspect as well.

You suggest all the members of the Court took the issue of homosexual marriage seriously, read the briefs, considered the arguments, and spent long hours pondering before reaching a decision—and so expect us to take *Obergefell* seriously?

I don't think so.

I am not expecting you to reply to the questions I have asked here. I am simply writing to urge you to retire yourself from the Court. You are not accountable—you don't have to explain or justify your decision—to a simple citizen like me.

You have decided that my state and I are required to recognize, to sanction, homosexual marriages and consider them "equal" to heterosexual marriages. You have delivered an opinion to that affect, and expect that what you have decided is the law on this matter. *Obergefell* should be applied and enforced as law. You are to be obeyed.

If you were wrong, if you made a mistake, if this "law" should not be a law; you are not accountable to a simple citizen like me. This is why the Constitution did not give the members of your branch of government the authority to tell simple citizens what the law is—that authority was given to a different branch of government which could be held accountable.

But I am compelled by curiosity to ask another question. Consider this a question from one man to another, rather than a mere citizen to a judge; and reply if you can find the time, because I would really like to know what you think about this one.

How would you explain what you have done with our Constitution, exemplified by *Obergefell,* to one of the Founding Fathers?

Imagine you are sitting across the table from one of the founders who put his life and the lives of his family, everything he had, at risk when he signed the Declaration of Independence. He went on and labored with others to deliver the Constitution, from which they created our government—a document which changed the world.

Imagine Benjamin Franklin is sitting across the table from you. I believe he was one of a handful who signed both documents.

You may also recall that as he was leaving the Constitutional Convention, Franklin was asked what kind of government the American people had been given, and he replied, "A republic, if you can keep it."

So imagine Benjamin Franklin asks what you, what the Supreme Court—what you did with the Constitution he and the others gave us.

You would want to explain, of course, that we ended slavery as practiced in his day. We did not do all we should have done when we should have done it; but we eventually created laws and recognized the basic rights that black people were entitled to as Americans.

You might explain that we carried on to thrive as a nation, and generally abided by the Constitution for hundreds of years.

I think you would also have to admit that in these days, as you are sitting at that table, nearly all Americans have come to take the Constitution for granted.

In your review with Benjamin Franklin, I expect you would also detail a few of the most important Supreme Court opinions as well. These would have to include, among others, *Roe v. Wade* and *Obergefell v. Hodges* (your very own opinion).

Maybe I can narrow my question a bit more here—how would you explain what the Supreme Court did with these two decisions?

What do you think Franklin would think when you explained that we used the Constitution to give a woman a right to end the life of her baby before it is born? We added that right to those in the Bill of Rights which some of the founders didn't think we needed at all.

What do you think Franklin would think when you explained that you used the Constitution to give a man a right to have "sex" with another man; and even gave a man a right to marry another man? You gave men and women these rights, and they were able to force anyone who did not agree to recognize these rights to keep their mouths shut.

What do you think Franklin would think when you explained that you used the Constitution to give a man a right to "define and express [his] identity" as a woman? You gave a woman a right to "define and express [her] identity" as a man? You gave a boy a right to "define and express [his] identity" as a girl or a codfish?

Well now I've gone and asked too many questions.

I wonder how you would explain these things. I think you might have trouble getting Franklin to believe what you have done.

I do know that I would not want to have to explain these things to Benjamin Franklin or any of the founders. I wouldn't want to have to explain how I as an American citizen had allowed these things to happen either, particularly if I had said nothing about it when I still had a right to do so.

This would be too shameful and embarrassing for me to explain.

I've said more than enough here, Justice Kennedy.

You need not reply. Just retire yourself and spend the rest of your days fishing or playing chess.

I will spend the rest of mine doing everything I lawfully can to oppose the enforcement of your *Obergefell* opinion as law in my state and all other states which do not recognize homosexual marriages under their state laws.

Sincerely,
Terry A. Larson

ENDNOTES

INTRODUCTION

1. Socratesinthecity. "Peter Hitchens: The Rage Against God." YouTube. January 05, 2016. Accessed February 04, 2017. https://www.youtube.com/watch?v=FEJ_ dtN0QO8&feature=youtu.be.

2. Metaxas, Eric. *If You Can Keep It: The Forgotten Promise of American Liberty*. New York: Viking, 2016.

CHAPTER 1

1. The separation of church and state is referenced in a letter written by Thomas Jefferson. There is no separation of church and state in the Constitution. The First Amendment reads, "Congress shall make no law respecting an establishment of religion, or prohibiting the free expression thereof."

   According to the Constitution, there are to be no laws prohibiting the free expression of religion. Christians have a duty to "express their religion" through involvement in politics and government.

It is simply a lie to demand that Christians stay out of and not influence government because of the separation of church and state, and a wonder that so many Americans have accepted this.

We wouldn't have a Constitution or a government if religious people had not been involved in creating it.

CHAPTER TWO

1. Dannemeyer, William. *Shadow in the Land: Homosexuality in America*. San Francisco: Ignatius Press, 1989.
2. Gao, George. "U.S. Millennials More Likely to Support Censoring Offensive Statements About Minorities." Pew Research Center. November 20, 2015. Accessed February 04, 2017. http://www.pewresearch.org/fact-tank/2015/11/20/40-of-millennials-ok-with-limiting-speech-offensive-to-minorities/ft_15-11-19_speech/.

CHAPTER FOUR

1. "Gender Dysphoria" (PDF). American Psychiatric Association. Retrieved February 4, 2017.

CHAPTER FIVE

1. Legislatures, National Conference of State. "Same-Sex Marriage Laws." Same-Sex Marriage Laws. Accessed February 04, 2017. http://www.ncsl.org/research/human-services/same-sex-marriage-laws.aspx.

2. Merriam-Webster. Accessed February 04, 2017. https://www.merriam-webster.com/words-at-play/woty2015-top-looked-up-words-ism.

3. Stéphane Courtois, Nicolas Werth, Jean-Louis Panné, Andrzej Paczkowski, Karel Bartošek, and Jean-Louis Margolin. *The Black Book of Communism: Crimes, Terror, Repression.* Translated by Jonathan Murphy and Mark Kramer. Cambridge, MA: Harvard University Press, 1999, 4.

CHAPTER SIX

1. "Reichstag Fire Decree." Wikipedia. Accessed February 04, 2017. https://en.wikipedia.org/wiki/Reichstag_Fire_Decree.

2. "New Data: Code of Federal Regulations Expanding, Faster Pace under Obama." Competitive Enterprise Institute. August 12, 2014. Accessed February 04, 2017. https://cei.org/blog/new-data-code-federal-

regulations-expanding-faster-pace-under-obama.

3. "Reg Stats | Regulatory Studies Center | The George Washington University." Reg Stats | Regulatory Studies Center | The George Washington University. Accessed February 04, 2017. https://regulatorystudies.columbian.gwu.edu/reg-stats#Total Pages in the Code of Federal Regulations (1936 - 2013).

4. Silverglate, Harvey A. *Three felonies a day: how the feds target the innocent.* New York: Encounter Books, 2009.

5. "HITLER SPEECH ON ENABLING ACT 1933." HITLER SPEECH ON ENABLING ACT 1933. Accessed February 04, 2017. http://www.worldfuturefund.org/Reports2013/hitlerenablingact.htm.

6. Shirer, William L. *The rise and fall of the Third Reich: a history of Nazi Germany.* New York: MJF Books, 1998.

7. Ibid., 38.

8. Ibid., 120.

9. Ibid., 121.

10. "Avalon Project : Nazi Conspiracy and Aggression - Volume 2 Chapter XV Part 6." Avalon Project : Nazi Conspiracy and Aggression - Volume 2 Chapter XV Part 6.

Accessed February 04, 2017. http://avalon. law.yale.edu/imt/chap15_part06.asp.

11. CBS/AP. "Pigs in a blanket" chant at Minnesota fair riles police." CBS News. August 31, 2015. Accessed February 04, 2017. http://www.cbsnews.com/news/pigs-in-a-blanket-chant-at-minnesota-fair-riles-police/.

12. "Open Syllabus Explorer beta 0.4." The Open Syllabus Project. Accessed February 04, 2017. http://explorer.opensyllabusproject.org/.

13. "Characteristics of U.S. Abortion Patients in 2014 and Changes Since 2008." Guttmacher Institute. June 10, 2016. Accessed February 13, 2017. https://www.guttmacher.org/report/characteristics-us-abortion-patients-2014#full-article.

14. Lepage, Jean-Denis. *Hitler Youth, 1922–1945: an illustrated history*. Jefferson, NC: McFarland & Company, 2009.

15. Ibid., 83.

16. "Frederick Douglass Project Writings: What Shall Be Done with the Slaves If Emancipated? | RBSCP." Frederick Douglass Project Writings: What Shall Be Done with the Slaves If Emancipated? | RBSCP. Accessed February 04, 2017. http://rbscp.lib.rochester.edu/4386.

17. "Nazi Medical Experiments." United States Holocaust Memorial Museum. Accessed February 04, 2017. https://www.ushmm.org/wlc/en/article.php?ModuleId=10005168.
18. Ibid.
19. Snyder, Timothy. *Black earth: the Holocaust as history and warning.* New York: Tim Duggan Books, 2015.
20. Ibid., 22.

CHAPTER SEVEN

1. "The Truth About Jim Crow." The American Civil Rights Union. Accessed February 04, 2017. http://www.theacru.org/jimcrow/.
2. "Immigrants in the United States." Center for Immigration Studies. Accessed February 04, 2017. http://cis.org/Immigrants-in-the-United-States#frontpage.
3. "Bibi Wilhailm - You are destroying Germany! 16 y o girl sheds light upon the refugee crisis." YouTube. January 22, 2016. Accessed March 07, 2017. https://www.youtube.com/watch?v=ZjBKYDEJDJk.
4. "Ohrdruf." United States Holocaust Memorial Museum. Accessed February 04, 2017. https://www.ushmm.org/wlc/en/article.php?ModuleId=10006131.

5. Chan, Jodi Rudoren and Sewell. "E.U. Move to Label Israeli Settlement Goods Strains Ties." The New York Times. November 11, 2015. Accessed March 07, 2017. https://www.nytimes.com/2015/11/12/world/middleeast/eu-labels-israeli-settlements.html?_r=0.

6. Fund, John. "The Facts about Mass Shootings." National Review. February 21, 2015. Accessed March 07, 2017. http://www.nationalreview.com/article/335739/facts-about-mass-shootings-john-fund.

CHAPTER EIGHT

1. Of course an unborn baby has a right to life. The unborn baby is alive. Every American citizen who lives in this country has a right to life. Every citizen has an interest in protecting that right, wants a government which will maintain and enforce that right, whether or not they are too lazy or apathetic to concern themselves with that right and only take it for granted.

Acknowledging an unborn baby has a right to life is moving in the right direction, is recognizing and elevating that right. Limiting the right to life, only because ascribing the right to life to an unborn baby might conflict with a woman's *right to end that life*, is moving in the wrong direction.

There are those who deny that an unborn baby has a right to life. It is generally those same people who demand all manner of other rights. If these people won't take the fundamental right to life itself seriously enough to ascribe it to an unborn baby, their demands for other rights should be disregarded and all their endless, mindless bellowing ignored.

If they won't grow up and place the kind of value we should place on every human life, protecting that life even before birth, we shouldn't take seriously their claims to higher moral ground as a result of their efforts to provide rights to people who enter the country illegally, who want social approval to engage in perverse and abnormal sexual behavior, or who want to fully realize their insanity by changing their sex or gender.

When the life of an unborn baby is at risk, when that life is discardable, then all of our lives are at risk.

2.   Wetzstein, Cheryl. "APA to correct manual: Pedophilia is not a 'sexual orientation'." The Washington Times. October 31, 2013. Accessed March 07, 2017. http://www.

washingtontimes.com/news/2013/oct/31/
apa-correct-manual-clarification-pedophilia-
not-se/.

CHAPTER NINE

1. egocentric. Dictionary.com. *Dictionary.
   com Unabridged.* Random House,
   Inc. http://www.dictionary.com/browse/
   egocentric (accessed: March 9, 2017).

2. After reading early excerpts of this book,
   a young mother suggested I might be
   exaggerating about sex education for five-
   year-olds; so I thought I would cite a few
   articles in the Notes at the end of the book.
   However, I think the results of a few Internet
   searches, shown in the following table, are
   more telling. Terms I searched for using
   Google, and the resulting number of page
   hits are shown.
   I began my search using "angry parents."
   The results are not for pages referencing
   "angry parents" who were demanding sex
   education or anti-bullying education for
   their children. The results are for pages
   referencing parents who became angry after
   discovering what progressive educators,
   homosexual activists, and other deviants
   were teaching their children in government

schools. The news stories and articles include plenty of references to children who were five-years-old, and some who were younger.

This is something which should not have been allowed—not only for kids as young as five years of age—it should not have been allowed for kids of *any* age in government schools.

SEARCH TERMS	RESULTS
"angry parents" + school + gay + children + five-year-old	51,300
"angry parents" + school + gay + children + sex	49,700
"angry parents" + school + gay + children + anti-bullying	30,500
"angry parents" + school + children + "gender identity"	7,920

CHAPTER TEN

1. "FBI Finds It Frequently Overstepped in Collecting Data." The Washington Post. June 14, 2007. Accessed March 07, 2017. http://www.washingtonpost.com/wp-dyn/content/article/2007/06/13/AR2007061302453.html.

2.   Evans, Dave. *The Internet Of Things: How The Next Evolution Of The Internet Is Changing Everything.* 1st ed. San Jose, CA: Cisco IBSG, 2017. Web. 9 Mar. 2017.

APPENDIX
MY RESPONSE TO OBERGFELL

1.   "HIV Among Gay and Bisexual Men." Centers for Disease Control and Prevention. September 30, 2016. Accessed January 30, 2017. https://www.cdc.gov/hiv/group/msm/index.html.

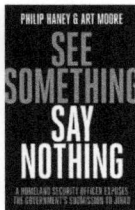

www.ingramcontent.com/pod-product-compliance
Lightning Source LLC
Chambersburg PA
CBHW030920090426
42737CB00007B/262